# ENDORSEMENTS

Dr. Watson challenges us to prepare ourselves for the uncertainties of life. Every strategy in the game plan is insightful, provocative, and Bible-based. He writes from his heart as he shares from his personal experiences and faith struggles. *Maximize Your Edge: Navigating Life's Challenges* charts the course for progressing from expectation to "making your move" in order to realize your dreams and achieve your goals.

**—Rev. Dr. Millicent Hunter, Chief Apostle, Pastor, Teacher**
The Baptist Worship Center
Worship Center Worldwide Fellowship of Churches

Lance Watson, one of the finest pastoral leaders in the United States, holds a steady compass for helping many to navigate the stormy currents of change and transition in our accelerated, postmodern culture. In the "crossover" tradition of John Maxwell, this book is practical, energetic, and clear. It will find a home not only on the bedside devotional table, but also in corporate offices, where leaders are learning that motivation is ultimately a spiritual matter.

**—Dr. John P. Chandler, Director of Evangelism and Church Growth**
Virginia Baptist Mission Board, Richmond, Virginia

In these wonderful, Spirit-saturated pages, Lance Watson has given us a spiritual TripTik to guide us into our destiny. Whoever reads and heeds his insightful words is sure to experience a more fulfilling life. Simple, pointed, clear, his insights leave no blur to cloud your vision of how to seize your future.

**—Dr. James C. Perkins, Pastor**
Greater Christ Baptist Church, Detroit, Michigan

Lance Watson's book is timely and to the point of real need. This work is, for today's awesome rate of personal changes, a Bible-based, practical-life parallel to the manuals we constantly use to operate our speedy PCs. One dares not venture into either new area without the best of advice.

**—Dr. Henry H. Mitchell**
Author of *Black Preaching: The Recovery of a Powerful Art, Preaching for Black Self-Esteem,* and *Celebration and Experience in Preaching*

To know Lance Watson is to be endeared to him; this book is the man in written form. While Lance's energy for God is difficult to contain on the printed page, the "gospel according to Lance" is emphatic and inspiring.

**—Kim Miller, Creative Director**
Ginghamsburg United Methodist Church, Tipp City, Ohio

I invite you to read this book with mental alertness and intellectual curiosity. Consider the content with spiritual seriousness. Among other things, Dr. Watson helps us to discover afresh that the devil is waging war against the church with renewed vigor. Dr. Lance Watson places us on the Avenue of Assurance: Prayer, Preparedness, and Participation. He speaks not only from profound explanation, but also from personal experiences. Listen to his heartbeat.

—**Dr. Frederick G. Sampson II, Senior Pastor**
Tabernacle Missionary Baptist Church, Detroit, Michigan

In *Maximize Your Edge: Navigating Life's Challenges*, Lance D. Watson has written a helpful prescription for getting old gracefully—or better still, how to get older without getting old. Timely, thoughtful, trenchant.

—**Dr. Gardner Taylor, Pastor Emeritus**
Concord Baptist Church of Christ, Brooklyn, New York

Lance Watson has written an invaluable book for young professionals. It combines common sense with practical principles and a deep sense of spirituality. It is truly a welcome relief to see a book helping persons to succeed where the emphasis is put on God and not on financial prosperity!

—**Rev. Dr. Jeremiah A. Wright, Jr., Senior Pastor**
Trinity United Church of Christ, Chicago, Illinois

Lance D. Watson is preeminently qualified to write about practical principles for living. He is a superb preacher whose preaching reflects a passion for the pragmatic. While his church has experienced and benefited from the dynamic leadership, teaching, and preaching of Lance Watson, the publication of this book will propel his voice and passion into a wider orbit.

—**Dr. Jason Barr, Pastor**
Macedonia Baptist Church, Philadelphia, Pennsylvania

Lance is a leader who knows how to inspire. This is a book that I will reread in those hard life seasons for the purpose of renewing a passionate life focus.

—**Rev. Michael Slaughter, Pastor**
Ginghamsburg United Methodist Church, Tipp City, Ohio
Author of *Unlearning Church*

# MAXIMIZE YOUR EDGE

navigating life's challenges

# MAXIMIZE YOUR EDGE

navigating life's challenges

# LANCE D. WATSON

ω

WHITAKER
HOUSE

Unless otherwise indicated, all Scripture quotations are from the *New King James Version,* © 1979, 1980, 1982 by Thomas Nelson, Inc. Used by permission. All rights reserved. Scripture quotations marked (NIV) are from the Holy Bible, *New International Version,* © 1973, 1978, 1984 by the International Bible Society. Used by permission. Scripture quotations marked (KJV) are taken from the King James Version of the Bible. Scripture quotations marked (NLT) are taken from the Holy Bible, *New Living Translation,* © 1996. Used by permission of Tyndale House Publishers, Inc., Wheaton, Illinois 60189. All rights reserved. Scripture quotations marked (TLB) are from *The Living Bible,* © 1971 by Tyndale House Publishers, Wheaton, Illinois. Used by permission. Scripture quotations marked (PHILLIPS) are from *The New Testament in Modern English,* © 1958, 1959, 1960, 1972 by J. B. Phillips, and © 1947, 1952, 1955, 1957 by The Macmillan Company.

## MAXIMIZE YOUR EDGE: NAVIGATING LIFE'S CHALLENGES

For more information on telecasts, conferences, products, and events featuring the author, contact Lance Watson on the World Wide Web at www.lancewatson.com, by mail at Positive Power Ministries, 2600 East Marshall Street, Richmond, Virginia 23223-7344, or by voicemail at (804) 643-4000.

ISBN: 0-88368-714-3
Printed in the United States of America
© 2001 by Lance D. Watson

Whitaker House
30 Hunt Valley Circle
New Kensington, PA 15068

Library of Congress Cataloging-in-Publication Data

Watson, Lance D., 1959–
    Maximize your edge: navigating life's challenges / Lance D. Watson.
       p.   cm.
    ISBN 0-88368-714-3 (pbk.: alk. paper)
    1. Christian life. I. Title.
    BV4501.3 .W38 2001
    248.4'861—dc21

                                      2001005428

2 3 4 5 6 7 8 9 10 11 12 13 14 / 10 09 08 07 06 05 04 03 02

# CONTENTS

# ACKNOWLEDGMENTS

The greatest blessing we receive on a daily basis is the gift of life—waking up each morning. After that, everything else is a bonus. I praise God for life, for my parents, and for the blessed memory of my grandparents.

I praise God for the wonderful partnership, rich friendship, and thrilling relationship that I share with my wife. Rose, our journey together is a masterpiece of matrimony. Thank you for the way you paint.

I praise God for my three children: Lance, Rachel, and Damon, in whose adoring eyes I see my best self, and in whose emerging possibilities my hope for tomorrow is restored. Daddy loves you.

For a loving, visionary, and supportive congregation called Saint Paul's, I am eternally grateful. Together we are "on the grow."

I am a product of every teacher who has ever taught me, every book I have ever read, and every school that has ever challenged me. Praise God for all of my teachers and mentors. Special thanks to Dr. Frederick G. Sampson, pastor of the Tabernacle Missionary Baptist Church in Detroit, Michigan, who met me at the crossroads and taught me to love knowledge: words are not enough. Thanks to Eric King and Patty Culbertson, who spent hours poring over this manuscript.

I make no claim of ownership or originality in these pages. What distinguishes them is that I have been able, by the grace of God, to prepare them for the ear and edit them for the eye. It is my hope and prayer that you will be encouraged and enriched as you read. Now is the time to *Maximize Your Edge* so that you will be successful in *Navigating Life's Challenges*.

# INTRODUCTION

Life is full of challenges: changing jobs, downsizing, outsourcing, advancements in technology, increased mobility, nurturing children, children leaving home, children coming home again—with their children, tackling tough relationships, separation, divorce, aging parents, growing older, retirement, coping with loss. Are you ready to navigate the challenges of life?

Like a raging river, challenges can either drown you or deliver you to your desired destination. It all depends on your ability to maximize your edge, navigate the turbulent rapids of life, and steer a clear course.

As we sail forward into this new millennium, we can anticipate unprecedented storms, immeasurable possibilities, and unlimited opportunities. Will you be ready? You need an edge! The insights that follow come from my struggles and successes in navigating the chaotic waters of life. You will be stimulated and hopefully encouraged to maximize your edge and get ready for the wild, wonderful experience that is the rest of your life.

If you need a game plan for the days ahead, if you want a strategy to conquer your circumstances, if you want a method to handle your hardships, read on. I invite you to share in the lessons I've learned from weaving my own tapestry of decisions day by day.

This work was originally designed as a series of sermons that I shared with the Saint Paul's Baptist Church family in Richmond, Virginia, where I am privileged to serve as their pastor. In these words, I hope you find living lessons from the heart of sacred Scripture that will empower you to *Maximize Your Edge* as you navigate life's obstacles and discover unexpected joy. If you're ready to put your boat in the water, turn the page.

# 1

# ELEVATE YOUR EXPECTATION

F aith is positive expectation. Faith is an attitude of abiding confidence. Faith is the oil that takes the friction out of living. The writer of Hebrews said, *"Faith is the substance of things hoped for, the evidence of things not seen"* (Heb. 11:1).

Faith is not desire; nor is it just wishing, hoping, and wanting something to take place. Intense desire can lead to faith, but faith is not merely desire. Faith is not pretending or engaging in what I've come to call "spiritual denial." Faith is not attempting— through repetition, chanting, or meditation—to "psyche" yourself up by saying, "I'm well! I'm well!" when, in actuality, you are struggling with sickness. These responses may be expressions of hope, but they are not faith.

Faith is also not merely a feeling; indeed, sometimes feelings are the exact opposite of faith. Faith is an attitude of abiding confidence: it is positive expectation. I believe that God has established irrefutable laws in the universe, and one of them is the law of expectation. The law of expectation is basically this: we tend to get what we expect out of life. We see what we expect to see, feel what we expect to feel, act how we expect to act, and achieve what we expect to achieve.

Our expectations influence the whole of our lives—our happiness, our health, our marriages, our careers, our relationships, and our abilities. I believe it, and Jesus taught it. In Matthew 9, we are privy to an episode in the life of Jesus during which a blind man seeking sight was healed. During this laser-less operation, Jesus said to him, *"According to your faith let it be to you"* (v. 29). What's the point? God has the power, but you and I must have faith—the positive expectation that God will work things out.

Permit me to rephrase this point: we get to choose how much God blesses us. Wow! We get to choose how rich our experiences of life will be. We get to choose our own boundaries, establish our own limitations, and determine our own successes in life.

As you contemplate your personal goals, dreams, plans, and aspirations, remember that you get to choose. The choice is not preprogrammed, predestined, or made for you; you get to choose it. Jesus, the Man who knows more about living life than anybody who has ever lived, said, *"According to your faith let it be to you"* (Matt. 9:29, emphasis added). There are at least two basic paths and philosophies by which you can live your life. You can live by fear or by faith. You can live in optimism or pessimism.

**Faith is positive expectation.**

In the biblical narrative, one of the most beloved characters of all time was a man named Job. Job was noted for his personal piety and moral character, but a closer look seems to reveal that Job was also somewhat of a pessimist; to the extent that he was, he became a magnet for heartache.

In one instance during his devastating ordeal, Job said, *"The thing I greatly feared has come upon me"* (Job 3:25). Read that statement again, *"'The thing I greatly feared has come upon me.'* I feared it, and that's what happened." Even though Job loved God and obeyed His commands, he had focused on what he did not want to happen instead of concentrating on what he did want to occur.

Are you doing that in your life? Are you focusing on what you don't want, instead of concentrating on what you do want? Often we say things like, "I don't want to get a divorce. I don't want to become sick. I don't want to go bankrupt. I don't want to lose this sale. I don't want to be overweight. I don't want my heart to be broken." The problem with this mental process is that our energies are focused on what we don't want instead of on what we do want.

Paul, the preeminent evangelist of the New Testament, said, *"I know whom I have believed and am persuaded that He is able to keep what I have committed to Him until that Day"* (2 Tim. 1:12). Notice the phrase *"I have committed,"* which indicates that Paul focused his energies on what he wanted. Paul refused to fix his focus on his fears, but he chose to focus his attention, energy, and strength on achieving the goal he desired.

**Positive expectation = positive results.**

Paul's affirmation was this: what I expect to happen will happen! Paul's stance was that God was both willing and able to keep what he was willing to commit to Him. Paul was confident that what he expected to happen *would* happen. Now, at the risk of overstating my case, let me raise these questions with you: What are you expecting now? What are you expecting for the rest of your life?

In the church where I minister, from time to time, we have a number of women who (along with their husbands) are expecting children. As a result of their expectation, they are compelled by the mandate of love and the desire for good health to make some changes in their schedules, their diets, their habits, and their homes. The expectation of a child mandates the preparation of the parent. Expectation mandates preparation. In a broader sense, all of us are *expecting* something to take place today, tomorrow, next week, and so on.

Our expectations may be conscious or unconscious, positive or negative, fear centered or faith based, but we all share this attitude: we're expecting something. My goal is to challenge you as you read these pages to *elevate the level of your expectation.* I want to challenge you to consciously choose the positive. No matter what you're going through, I challenge you to positively expect that your life will get better.

As the faithful in the church of my childhood used to sing, so we must believe that "there is a bright side somewhere." As the prophet Isaiah reassured the people of Israel, we must trust that *"no weapon formed against [us] shall prosper"* (Isa. 54:17), and that, somehow, God will make a way. We must possess positive expectation.

One of the most dynamic illustrations of positive expectation in the heart of sacred Scripture is found in the classic confrontation of David and Goliath. Even if you are well acquainted with all of the details of this drama, may I encourage you not to let your familiarity with the story rob you of its gripping message?

**Expectation mandates preparation.**

This stirring story provides for us some practical yet powerful steps on how to elevate the level of expectancy in our lives, as we seek to maximize our edge. The epic unfolds in the Old Testament book of 1 Samuel. Goliath, Israel's nemesis, was a giant from Gath, a neighboring, antagonistic nation. He was reported to be over nine feet tall and wore a couple hundred pounds of bronze armor. He was the "Heavyweight Champion of Palestine"—the best pound-for-pound fighter of his era. His threats had immobilized the armies of Israel, and they cowered in terror before him.

Each day, Goliath would walk out on the battlefield and shout, "Send out your best man. I'll fight him, and whoever wins the scrimmage wins the battle." (See 1 Samuel 17:8–10.) Everybody was frightened to death! The Scripture reports: *"When Saul and all Israel heard these words of the Philistine, they were dismayed and greatly afraid"* (v. 11).

At this point, the story turns. Just back from tending sheep on the "back forty," David appeared. He was a young teenager at the time, and in that brash courage that characterizes adolescence, David said, "I'm not afraid. I'll fight the giant. I have *'killed both lion and bear; and this uncircumcised Philistine will be like one of them, seeing he has defied the armies of the living God'* (1 Sam. 17:36)." Notice immediately the level and intensity of his confidence. Notice the level of his expectation.

David, addressing King Saul, said, *"Let no man's heart fail because of him; your servant will go and fight with this Philistine"* (v. 32). Whatever else we might say about David, we are compelled to say this: he was confident. Rejecting the king's armor, David *"chose for himself five smooth stones from the brook, and put them in a shepherd's bag, in a pouch which he had, and his sling was in his hand"* (v. 40).

As the epic unfolds, the writer provides us with the basis and reason for David's confidence. From the lips of David came these words, soaked in grateful memory: *"The LORD, who delivered me from the paw of the lion and from the paw of the bear, He will deliver me from the hand of this Philistine"* (v. 37).

David's affirmation was this: I'm confident *now* because the Lord delivered me *then.* The Lord Almighty is the Source of my positive expectation. David expected a positive outcome because of the God he served. David's perspective on the present problem was based on his knowledge of past deliverance. God had delivered him in the past; therefore, he expected God to deliver him in the present.

How we deal with our problems, face our difficulties, and tackle our traumas is all a matter of perspective. Every soldier cowering in fear in that valley shared a common conviction: "That guy's too big to hit! We'll never be able to kill him." David looked over the ledge and said, "He's too big to miss!" The difference was David's perspective.

Most of us are familiar with the end of the story. David took on Goliath in a one-on-one battle. David *"ran"* (v. 48) out into the valley, and parenthetically, this is the way to face your challenges: run *to* them, not *from* them. There's no need to hesitate when you're confident of a positive outcome. David *"ran"* into the valley, fought Goliath, and won the day.

## Expecting the Best Honors God

There are some powerful lessons here for each of us as we embrace this new millennium and get ready for the rest of our lives. As we live in a posture of positive expectation, as we expect the best, we honor God.

David said to Goliath in this confrontation,

> *This day the LORD will deliver you into my hand, and I will strike you and take your head from you. And this day I will give the carcasses of the camp of the Philistines to the birds of the air and the wild beasts of the earth.* (1 Sam. 17:46)

David's description was brutal; but given the odds, it was a completely courageous affirmation. What was David doing through his dialogue with Goliath? He was painting mental pictures. With his words, he was helping Goliath to see things as he saw them. David was planting a thought in Goliath's mind and helping him to visualize the desired outcome.

**It is a tribute to God when we expect great things from Him.**

I can hear David saying, "Goliath, this is what I'm going to do to you. You're going to be chopped liver. *'Then all this assembly shall know that the LORD does not save with sword and spear; for the battle is the Lord's, and He will give you into our hands'* (v. 47)."

Now that's positive expectation! An adolescent struggling with puberty and pimples made this statement to a giant *before* anything happened: "Victory belongs to me." He expected the best. Nothing honors God more than our great expectations.

I have been blessed to have three children, and when they approach me *expectantly*, it raises my level of responsibility. It also raises the level of my esteem. I find myself saying, "They really believe in me. They really trust me. They really think I can do anything." Their clear expectation encourages me to do *more* than I would have done and to go *further* than I would have gone.

When we declare by our lips and our lives, "My God can do anything!" that posture and proclamation of positive expectation honors God. It's a testimony based on our faith in God. The writer of Hebrews reminded believers in the early church, *"Without faith it is impossible to please Him, for he who comes to God must believe that He is, and that He is a rewarder of those who diligently seek Him"* (Heb. 11:6).

## Expecting the Best Increases Ability

What are you expecting right now in your life? It is a tribute and a testimony to the God you love and who loves you, for you to say in advance, "I'm expecting great things." Positive expectation honors God, and it increases your ability.

Every athlete knows that a positive attitude is critical in any contest. Positive attitude is the winning edge. Athletes who expect to win do far better on a performance level than athletes who expect to lose. Muhammad Ali, arguably the most prominent heavyweight fighter of the twentieth century, lost only two fights in his life prior to his first retirement.

Both of those fights had one thing in common: before the fight he gave a press conference and made a statement, "If I should lose this fight...." *If* is a word of doubt. Could it be that he set himself up to lose the only two fights he ever lost prior to his first retirement? You be the judge, but don't miss the point. As we act in faith, we receive additional strength. Supernatural power is made available.

Go back to 1 Samuel 17. The Bible says,

> *So it was, when the Philistine arose and came and drew near to meet David, that David hastened and ran toward the army to meet the Philistine. Then David put his hand in his bag*

*and took out a stone; and he slung it and struck the Philistine
in his forehead.* (vv. 48–49)

Only Goliath's forehead was not covered by his armor.

David was expectant, and that fueled his ability. He believed that
God would provide; and acting upon that expectation, he achieved
his objective. Some people say that David lacked faith because he
took five rocks for one giant. Read further. Second Samuel 21:22
tells us that Goliath had four brothers. David was prepared for
the whole family! I imagine he said to himself, "I'm not just going
to knock this one 'buster' off, but if I have to—I'm ready for the
whole family. C'mon out here. I've got a rock for each one of you!"

Expecting the best from God increases our ability. Never use lack
of ability as an excuse for a lack of production. Statements like, "I
can't do it," "I'm too old," or "I'm too young" are both untrue and
unproductive. As my grandmother used to say, "Age ain't nothing
but a number." God can compensate for any deficiency if we possess a high level of expectation. Never let an impossible situation
intimidate you. Let it motivate you.

## Today's impossibilities are tomorrow's miracles.

If you ever use the word *impossible* again,
listen for a laugh from heaven. *Impossible*
is not in God's vocabulary. God increases our ability when we expect Him
to work in our lives. Dismiss your
doubts. David did not make excuses; he
made plans. David expected God to work.

The Scriptures are replete with instances of people who made excuses. Moses said, "I can't speak." He told the Lord, *"I am not elo-
quent, neither before nor since You have spoken to Your servant; but I
am slow of speech and slow of tongue"* (Exod. 4:10). Jeremiah said,
"I'm too young." He told God, *"I cannot speak, for I am a youth"* (Jer.
1:6). Amos said, "I'm uneducated." He said, *"I was no prophet, nor
was I a son of a prophet, but I was a sheepbreeder and a tender of syca-
more fruit"* (Amos 7:14). Others have said, "I'm too old." Don't use

your lack of ability as an excuse. Our extremity is God's opportunity. Expecting the best honors God. Expecting the best increases ability.

## Expecting the Best Encourages Others

Optimism, enthusiasm, and faith are contagious. In 1 Samuel 17, we read, *"David ran and stood over the Philistine, took his sword and drew it out of its sheath and killed him, and cut off his head with it. And when the Philistines saw that their champion was dead, they fled"* (v. 51).

Look at the attitude change in the Israelite army. *"Now the men of Israel and Judah arose and shouted, and pursued the Philistines as far as the entrance of the valley and to the gates of Ekron"* (v. 52). Everybody suddenly became courageous and joined the winner! Everybody got his confidence back; they all were motivated and inspired by David's example. Expecting the best encourages others because enthusiasm and optimism are contagious.

Last year we had a tremendous celebration in our church. Over 1300 families pledged millions of dollars toward the construction of our new campus. When we announced that God had moved on people's hearts in that miraculous way, everybody was excited. Since that time, I have talked with many first-time visitors who say, "I want to be a member of this church! This is exciting. Something's going on here." What's the point? Everybody wants to be a part of a winning team. Everybody wants to be on the train called "success."

Enthusiasm and faith are contagious. Our church is an encouragement to other churches. Expecting the best builds enthusiasm and confidence in the lives of others. Perhaps as you read this testimony, you are saying, "I wish I had that kind of faith, but I'm a born pessimist! I'm naturally negative." Perhaps you are inclined always to see the problem and never the possibility. Maybe you have a natural tendency to look on the downside, rather than the upside. You may be the type of person who sees each cup as half empty, rather than half full; however, there's hope for you!

You can develop a positive personality. How? Work at it. If you are a naturally negative person, you have to work at building your faith and increasing your optimism. We all have different personalities. Some of us are firecrackers, and some of us are duds. No matter what you are now, remember this: optimism is a choice. You choose how much you want to believe God.

Five principles from God's Word can assist you. Putting these five elements into practice will help you to develop a positive personality, to increase your faith, to elevate the level of expectation in your life, and to gain an attitude of positive expectancy. You are en route to enthusiasm. You are on the way to a dynamic life. I dare you to read on!

## Start Your Day with Faith

Every day when you open your eyes, try this affirmation, "Goodbye, doubt. You are free to leave now." Dismiss your doubt, and start your day with faith. In Psalm 5:3, we find one of the keys that built David's faith, elevated the level of his expectation, and propelled his personal possibility. David said, *"Listen to my voice in the morning, LORD. Each morning I bring my requests to you and wait expectantly"* (NLT).

I start my day with faith and not doubt. Do you naturally wake up happy in the morning, or do you wake up a little grumpy?

The story is told of a guy who was out on the street conducting interviews. He approached a couple and said, "Excuse me, sir. Do you wake up grouchy in the morning?" The man looked over at his wife and said, "No, I usually let her sleep." Here's the point: every day when we get up, we can choose one of two attitudes: "Good morning, Lord!" or "Good Lord! It's morning!"

How is it for you? Are you naturally pessimistic? Do you wake up that way? Do you remember Eeyore, the old donkey in A. A. Milne's *Winnie-the-Pooh*? He epitomizes pessimism. Even Pooh can't convince him that the new day is going to be good. He is focused on how he looks and how little anyone really cares. His attitude can be summed up in one of his favorite words: *pathetic.*[1]

Some of us are like Eyeore. We wake up with a doubtful, pessimistic attitude. I encourage you to start your day with faith, not doubt. Start each morning with positive expectation. As you wake up, take a moment and say to yourself, "This is going to be a great day! *'This is the day the LORD has made; [I] will rejoice and be glad in it'* (Ps. 118:24)." Start the day with the Lord. Start with good news—not with bad news. Don't start with the negative; start with the positive.

## Look for the Positive

Listen to cheerful music. Put on an inspirational tape on the way to work. Read a Scripture. Memorize a promise. Talk to the Lord. Have a quiet time. Start with positive input in your life, and that sets the tone for the rest of your day. If you begin with positive expectations, you will feel better.

Lionel Tiger, in his book *Optimism: The Biology of Hope*, writes about the research that has been conducted that indicates that optimism—positive expectation—creates endorphins in the brain.[2] Endorphins are the chemicals that reduce pain and produce a feeling of well-being. Optimism actually creates well-being in your body. It causes the nerves, the neurons in your mind, to release the chemical that produces that feeling of well-being. Start the morning with God. Stop waiting to have a good day, and start *making* it a good day. It's a choice. Find good everywhere.

Our expectations are elevated when we determine to look for the good in everything and everybody. Romans 8:28 says, *"And we know that all things work together for good to those who love God, to those who are the called according to His purpose."* All things don't work together for good for everybody. All things work together for good for those who love God and who are trying to live in God's purpose.

Look for something good in everything and everyone. Emphasize the positive; that will raise your expectation level. One writer said, "Things turn out best for those who make the best of the way things turn out." Am I asking you to be unrealistic, to ignore your problems? Not at all.

We can be realistic and optimistic at the same time. We can recognize problems without rehearsing them over and over. We don't pretend that nothing is wrong or that everything is perfect. We don't ignore our problems. We just realize that, with God's help, we can handle them, and we expect God to help.

> **God specializes in bringing good out of bad situations.**

In Psalm 5:3, David offered us an example of this type of response when he said, *"Listen to my voice in the morning, LORD. Each morning I bring my requests to you and wait expectantly"* (NLT). Note his incredible attitude. In Psalm 18, David revealed the outlook that is produced when we are optimistic. His attitude was: with God's help, I can handle any problem.

In Psalm 18:28, David said, *"'You, O LORD, keep my lamp burning; my God turns my darkness into light'* (NIV). You keep me consistent. I don't run out of energy. You turn problems into possibilities, You turn obstacles into opportunities, and You turn darkness into light." David continued, *"With your help I can advance against a troop; with my God I can scale a wall"* (v. 29 NIV). I can take them on at the office. I can handle all the critics. In the Hebrew language, the phrase, *"I can advance against a troop,"* literally means, "I can run through a barricade."

What confidence! What positive expectation! Yes, there will be problems, but you can handle them with God's help. You *"can do all things through Christ who strengthens [you]"* (Phil. 4:13). Indeed, we are told, *"Count it all joy when you fall into various trials"* (James 1:2). Problems are friends! Some of us have a lot of friends! Don't deny your problems; defy your problems.

David defied his problem. He didn't say, "Let's pretend that guy doesn't exist out there on the battlefield." He recognized Goliath's threat as a legitimate problem, yet he defied him in the name of God and said, *"I come to you in the name of the LORD"* (1 Sam. 17:45). Look for something good in everything and everyone. Let your attitude be positive no matter what happens.

Pessimism is an insult to God. Whenever we permit ourselves to be pessimistic, we offer up a prayer that says, "God, I really doubt that You care or that You're strong enough to handle the problems in this particular situation." Pessimists are always looking backward. They never look to the future. In essence, what they are saying is, "It's never worked before. Nobody else has ever done it. It's never worked out in the past." They're programming themselves to repeat history because that's where they're focused.

> **A pessimistic believer is a contradiction in terms.**

## Watch Your Words

Ephesians 4:29 conveys this poignant principle by encouraging us in this way: *"Let no corrupt word proceed out of your mouth* [not tearing others down, but building them up], *but what is good for necessary edification* [not according to your needs, but to theirs], *that it may impart grace to the hearers* [not that it may benefit you]."

Words are a powerful force in our lives. Words have tremendous influence. If we are ever going to learn to live by faith, we must watch the way we talk. May I suggest three phrases that each of us should work to eliminate from our vocabularies?

### What If

"What if" is a statement of doubt, not a statement of faith. One time a man came to Jesus to ask for healing for his son. He said to Jesus, *"If You can do anything..."* (Mark 9:22). Jesus said to him, *"If you can believe, all things are possible to him who believes"* (v. 23, emphasis added). The word *if* did not apply to Jesus. Many times you hear people say things, such as, "If my marriage doesn't work out…"; "If the project doesn't fly…"; "If this job doesn't work out…." The problem with this type of skepticism is that we are virtually guaranteeing failure. Success requires a 100-percent commitment. Eliminate the phrase "what if" as much as possible. "What if" is a phrase of failure, a clause of doubt.

### I Can't

There is a big difference between saying, "I can't" and "I won't"; "I can't" and "I don't want to"; "I can't" and "It's not a priority for me"; or "I can't" and "It's not God's will." To say the words *I can't* is a contradiction of Philippians 4:13, which says, *"I can do all things through Christ who strengthens me."*

### Yes, But

When someone says, "Yes, but," he often means, "I don't really want to change. I don't really want to grow. I don't really want any help; I just want pity."

As much as possible, eliminate these negative phrases from your thinking and your conversation. Watch your words.

## Keep Company with Positive People

Translated another way, this principle would read: avoid complainers. First Corinthians 15:33 says, *"Bad company corrupts good character"* (NIV). Over and over again in the Scriptures we're taught to watch our relationships and friendships because they have such a profound influence on our lives. People who are constantly negative—putting us down, being critical, nagging, complaining, always looking at the wrong things and saying what's wrong—should not be our preferred companions. If you are naturally a negative person, the best thing in the world you could do is surround yourself with optimistic people. Optimism rubs off. That's one of the tremendous benefits of active participation in the church. It affords us the opportunity to be around positive people.

Hebrews 13:7 says, *"Remember your leaders, who spoke the word of God to you. Consider the outcome of their way of life and imitate their faith"* (NIV). If you want to be a leader in life, you have to become a positive person. One of the marks of leadership is that you will have a faith that other people will want to imitate. You will have a level of expectation, a positive attitude that declares, "It can be done!" An optimistic, faith-filled attitude is critical for strong leaders.

In Paul's first letter to Timothy, Paul suggested that there were people in the church who had an unhealthy interest in controversy and criticism, and who were argumentative. The Scriptures teach that people like that lack understanding and are to be avoided. Never participate in group griping. Criticism is as contagious as an airborne virus: it spreads very quickly. If somebody starts griping, everybody else joins in.

It is impossible to be critical and creative at the same time. Critical people talk things down; creative people build things up. An interesting feature appears in the story of Joshua as the Israelites prepared to raid the land that God had promised them. God instructed them to walk in a circle around the city of Jericho for seven days in absolute silence. There was to be no talking. Joshua told the people, *"You shall not shout or make any noise with your voice, nor shall a word proceed out of your mouth, until the day I say to you, 'Shout!'"* (Josh. 6:10).

**You cannot be critical and creative at the same time.**

Why were they not to talk? God knew it would take only a couple of cynics to ruin the whole thing. It would take only one or two complainers who would be walking around saying, "This plan is silly! It does not make sense. I feel like a fool." Then somebody else would say, "You're right! This is kind of foolish. We need to have a meeting and take a vote on the foolishness of this idea."

All of our lives are peppered with people who tend to see the pitfalls in every parade and the storm in every sky. In 1697, Thomas

Beverly, a rector in the Church of England, wrote a book predicting that the world would end in 1697. Then he wrote a second book in 1698 complaining that the world had ended in 1697, but nobody had noticed!

Many people face life with a similar attitude. They are "card carrying" members of the Henny Penny club. They sit around saying, "The sky is falling! Doom and gloom." There was a man and his wife, both well over 90 years old, whose 70-year-old son had died. Returning from the funeral service the old man said to his wife, "I told you we would never raise that boy!" That's a pessimist.

It's like the hypochondriac who had put on her tombstone, "I told you I was sick!" A friend said, "If I found a four-leaf clover, I'd probably hurt my back trying to pick it up." Too many people belong to Pessimists International. From where does negativity come? The root cause is fear. In the Garden of Eden, when Adam and Eve sinned, Adam said, *"I was afraid…; and I hid"* (Gen. 3:10).

Someone who is constantly negative is afraid. When we are insecure, we become defensive. When we are afraid and feel threatened, our walls go up. It is true in marriage; when people are afraid that their partners may walk out, they get defensive or angry. Anger is fear. If you push a cat back in the corner, it will back up until finally it cannot go any further; then it will attack. If you want to get rid of your negative tendency, you have to work on the root: fear. When you develop the confidence, security, and self-esteem that come from knowing Christ—from knowing that Christ cares for all your needs and that no problem is too significant for Him to handle—you will find your negative tendency waning.

**Fear is the darkroom where negatives develop.**

Ask God to help you with your fear. If you struggle with this problem, pray, "Lord, it's true. I tend to look at everything in the negative. I tend to see the wrong things. Help me." God will help you. Elevating the level of your expectancy will maximize your edge in life. It will make you better able to navigate life's challenges.

## Thank God in Advance

Does that advice sound strange to you? Usually we thank God *after* the fact, yet I want to challenge you even as you read this chapter to begin to thank God in advance. Thank God for *what you expect.* In Mark 11, there is a dynamic principle that suggests that we must expect an answer from God when we pray. If we do not expect God to answer, we should not pray. We must believe in advance.

Believing in advance is a practical principle that is taught throughout Scripture: you must believe; *then* you will receive. You must believe in advance. "You mean I have to believe that it's already here before I get it?" Yes! If you believe after you have received, is that faith? No, that's gratitude.

In Mark 11:22–24, Jesus says,

> *Have faith in God. For assuredly, I say to you, whoever says to this mountain, "Be removed and be cast into the sea," and does not doubt in his heart, but believes that those things he says will be done, he will have whatever he says. Therefore, I say to you, whatever things you ask when you pray, believe that you receive them, and you will have them.*

Faith is thanking God in advance. Jesus gave us an example of this truth when He prayed for Lazarus to be brought back from the dead. Jesus walked up to the tomb where Lazarus had been buried. He did not ask or beg God to raise Lazarus. Instead,

**Faith is believing a thing is so, even when it isn't—so that it might be.**

He prayed, *"Father, I thank You that You have heard Me."* That's

27

faith! In the next verse He said that He was praying that way *"because of the people who* [were] *standing by."* That's faith!

Faith is expecting the best and thanking God in advance. The power of expectation, the power of positive faith, can change your life. We do not always get what we deserve in life, but we do get what we expect. What are you expecting next week? A lab report from your doctor? Expect the best. Worrying will not make the results better. Expect the best.

Need to make a sale this week? Need to improve your job performance? Expect the best. Need to make a decision about your marriage? Expect God to work in you, with you, and through you. *"According to your faith let it be to you"* (Matt. 9:29). Nothing honors God more than when we elevate our expectation. Would you make a confession of positive expectation now in the presence of God?

## Prayer:

> Gracious God, thank You for the power of positive expectation. Starting here, starting now, I release my fears and all of my negative and defensive emotions. I thank You that right now I am accepted, loved, and supported by You. From this moment forward, I expect the best. I will begin this day with faith. I dismiss my doubt. I will look for the good in things and in people. I will not deny my problems, but by Your power, I will defy my problems and face them with positive expectation.
>
> Loving God, do surgery on my vocabulary. Help me to eliminate my complaints and extend my compliments. I rejoice in the victory that is life. Surround me with optimism. I thank You in advance that this is going to be the greatest week of my life. My faith is going to grow. My needs will be met. I'm getting stronger. In the mighty, miraculous, and matchless name of Jesus, I pray. Amen.

# 2

# ALTER YOUR ATTITUDE

O ur choice of attitude in life and toward life is absolutely criti-cal. Many times it is not what happens *to* us that determines the flow of our lives, but what happens *in* us. William James, who taught psychology and philosophy at Harvard University during the late 1800s, said, "The greatest discovery of my generation is that human beings can alter their lives by altering their attitudes of mind."[1] By changing your mind, you can change your life.

I believe that we all want good results from life—in our homes, in our work, and in all our contacts with other people. The tidbit of truth, the morsel of meaning, that I want to share with you is this: the single most important factor that will guarantee good results, day in and day out, is choosing to have a healthy attitude.

**Our attitudes toward life determine life's attitude toward us.**

Our attitudes tell the world what we expect. If we have cheerful, ex-pectant attitudes, they announce to everyone that we expect the best in our dealings with the world. We all tend to live up (or down, as the case may be) to our expectations.

If we're cheerful and glad to have experienced the miracle of life, others will respond to us in a similar way. We get back what we give out. Our surroundings are a mirror of who we are. *Things* can change because *we* can change, but nothing will change until we do. Attitudes are critically important: they are ultimately what drive us to act in a certain way. In describing the attitudes that worked to make him extremely successful across many years, a professional speaker said that people need to focus on two words: *gratitude* and *expectation.*

Gratitude—because to live on this beautiful and astonishing planet is a blessing. Expectation—because it empowers us to aim for the best, believe in our goals, and go to work on them. So many people live narrow, bitter, frustrated lives; they live defensively because they have adopted a pessimistic and ungrateful attitude toward life.

All of us will have challenges in life, but the person with a poor attitude becomes a magnet for the unpleasant. A bad attitude multiplies the negative experiences of life. Let me explain. If you live long enough, hard times will come. When hard times come, if you have chosen to have a bad attitude, a poor attitude, a pessimistic attitude, or a negative attitude, those hard times, those challenges, will reinforce, magnify, and intensify a negative, pessimistic perspective.

A negative attitude will make problems appear more powerful than they are, situations more stressful than they are, and obstacles more ominous than they are. Life will seem to be more difficult than it really is. A negative attitude will become a self-generating, doom-fulfilling prophecy. Bad things will happen not because you were predestined for them or because they were God's will for you, but because of your choice of attitude. As one writer said, "If you have onions on your breath, the whole world smells." It's all about your attitude.

It would be impossible to estimate the number of jobs lost, promotions forfeited, grades lowered, sales squandered, marriages ruined, and friendships fractured because of poor attitudes.

## We Get What We Expect

Our outlook on life is the paintbrush with which we color our world. Each one of us shapes his or her own life. The course and direction, the quality or lack of quality in our lives, are determined by our habitual choices of attitude. Change your attitude, and you change your life. Now that sounds simple, doesn't it? We all know that it is not quite that easy. Why? Altering our attitudes takes time. Once an attitude has become a habit, it takes effort, power, determination, and strength to change it.

In the Genesis narrative, we meet a man named Jacob who was in the midst of an attitude alteration. His story reveals how God works with us and in us to change our attitudes from hurtful to helpful, from negative to positive, from demonic to delightful. In Genesis 32–33, it's evident that God has been at work slowly but surely in the life

**Change your attitude, and you will change your life.**

of Jacob to transform his attitude *toward* life and *in* life.

For more than twenty years, Jacob's life had been characterized and dominated by deceit and selfishness. Jacob wanted what he wanted; he worked, schemed, connived, and manipulated to get what he wanted, even at the expense of others.

In the tradition of Hebrew families, every child was entitled to an inheritance. The oldest child was given a *"double portion"* (Deut. 21:17), called his birthright. In addition, the oldest child also received a *blessing* from his father, which legally made him heir and gave him supervision over the entire family when the parent passed on. In Jacob's family, the birthright and the blessing belonged to Esau. As the oldest son, Esau had rightful claim to both, yet Jacob found a way to take them away from him.

Conspiring with his mother, Jacob robbed Esau of both his birthright and his blessing. (See Genesis 27.) In many circumstances, blood is thicker than water—until you add money and sex to the mix.

As a side note, I would like to interject two points. First, I believe that parents should determine in their hearts that they are going to live in such a way as to leave their children an inheritance. Our children should be better off financially than we are, but that cannot happen if we fail to manage faithfully and wisely what God has given to us or if we fail to teach our children how to do likewise.

**Pray about it.**
**Produce it.**
**Protect it.**
**Pass it on.**

Here's a formula for financial deliverance: pray about it, produce it, protect it, and pass it on. Parents should determine to leave their children not just a financial inheritance, but also an inheritance of faith, hope, love, and integrity.

Second, realize that we do not need to resent, envy, or be jealous of the way God blesses others. Your blessing has your name on it. You don't have to steal somebody else's blessing. You don't have to scheme or manipulate your way. Instead, trust God. What God has for you is for you.

In Genesis 32, an angel engaged Jacob in a physical struggle. Even in the midst of this struggle, Jacob had the audacity to insist that he be given a blessing. For his entire adult life, Jacob's goal—his controlling attitude—had been one of arrogant, selfish, deceitful taking of what he wanted, whether it was rightfully his or not. In fact, even Jacob's name bore witness to this unpleasant character trait, for the name Jacob literally means "the supplanter," or one who steals the position and standing of another.

Jacob's parents, Isaac and Rebekah, gave this name to Jacob when he was born, because he came into the world clinging to the heel of his older brother, Esau, as if even then he was trying to "get ahead" of him. Jacob's parents could never have guessed how faithfully he would live up to his name. Jacob's attitude was selfish and deceitful, and his mother cultivated that attitude in him. What started in childhood continued into adulthood.

Much of what ails us today didn't start yesterday; it has its roots way back in our childhoods. The seed was planted then, and we are reaping the harvest now. That is what happened with Jacob. Years later, the tables were turned, and Jacob had to endure the scheming of his father-in-law, Laban.

Jacob had agreed to work for Laban for seven years for Rachel's hand in marriage, but on the morning after the wedding feast, Jacob discovered what the darkness had hidden. He had married Leah—Rachel's older sister. Jacob protested Laban's duplicity, but Laban said, *"It is not our custom here to give the younger daughter in marriage before the older one"* (Gen. 29:26). Just as Jacob had tricked Esau out of Esau's rightful blessing, the tables had been turned on Jacob. In order to take Rachel as his wife, he had to agree to another seven years of work.

Laban's flocks increased under Jacob's shepherding because God's blessing was on Jacob. After his fourteen years of service were ended, Jacob wanted to return to his homeland. He made a deal with Laban that he would continue to work for him in order to establish a flock of his own. He asked Laban for the speckled goats and the dark-colored sheep. Laban had no sooner agreed to the deal than he violated the terms. He secretly culled the flocks for the very sheep and goats that should have gone to Jacob. Perhaps God was allowing Jacob to experience firsthand the painful consequences of deceit.

In spite of Laban's efforts to thwart Jacob's success, Jacob had his own plan. He managed to breed the stock so that the best animals belonged to him, and the weaker ones went to Laban. Jacob told Rachel and Leah, *"God has taken away the livestock of your father and given them to me"* (Gen. 31:9). Jacob did what we so often do in attempting to cover our tracks: he declared it was God's will for things to happen the way they did. Many things that we do are not by divine design. Yet in the midst of Jacob's struggle, God did something he didn't expect: He altered Jacob's attitude and gave him a new name.

God renamed Jacob, *"Israel"* (Gen. 32:28), which means, "God strives." God's desire was to transform Jacob's outlook on life. Jacob had been living his entire life with the attitude that God owed him something, that God was somehow fighting against him to keep him from having what rightfully belonged to him. God's goal was to transform Jacob's attitude, to help him to see that He was not fighting *against* him, but was fighting *for* him.

What remained to be seen was whether the change would really take, because a bad attitude is hard to alter. People who are pessimistic tend to remain pessimists. People who are negative tend to remain negative. People who are lazy tend to keep being lazy. People who are conniving tend to stay that way. Attitudes are not just something we have; attitudes are a reflection of who we are.

Goethe, the great German philosopher, once said, "Before you can do something, you must first be something."[2] To a dull person, everything is dull. To a boring person, everything is boring. But to an excited person, everything is exciting. A loving person views life with a loving attitude. What we see is largely determined by who we are.

Many years ago, a newspaper reporter asked a famous Los Angeles restaurateur, "When did you become successful?" He replied, "I was successful even when I was flat broke. I knew what I wanted to do, and I knew I'd do it. It was only a matter of time." Before we can *do* something, we must *be* something.

That's what the wrestling is about in Genesis 32. What Jacob was had to be thrown down. What he was called had to be cast aside. How he walked had to be changed. Those are the three things that happened in that fight. The angel threw him down, changed his name, and touched him in the hollow of his hip so that Jacob left that encounter with a limp. He didn't walk out the same way he walked in. Before we go further, let's make this point clear: we're not only talking about Jacob; this message has our names on it, too.

This biblical lesson is more than just a study provoked by our curiosity about the pilgrimage of Jacob. Our footprints are in this passage. Our attitudes need adjustment every now and then. Our attitudes get knocked off track and need alteration. This is an opportune moment as you read this chapter to examine your heart. Take a good look at your thoughts, feelings, actions, and emotions because you may be in need of an attitude alteration. Frankly, all of us from time to time demonstrate attitudes of selfishness, arrogance, greed, impurity, hatred, and so many other things that harm our relationships, diminish our spiritual health, and impede our usefulness. Today represents our opportunity to experience an *attitude alteration.*

Just as Jacob was "thrown down and bounced around" in that wrestling match, sometimes God has to permit us to be thrown down and bounced around by our messes and mistakes. He allows these experiences not to hurt us, but to help us; not to crush us, but to change us; not to annihilate us, but to anchor us so that we will walk differently coming out of the experience than we did going in.

God renamed Jacob with a name meaning, "God strives" or "God fights." We serve a God who fights for us and stands with us. God has blessed us. God has given us ultimate victory. God is blessing us right now.

**God is on your side.**

Jacob's attitude appeared to be altered, but the challenge was yet to come. A car's abilities are not fully seen on the showroom floor, a boat in the harbor is not demonstrating its full capabilities, and a new attitude is not authentically ours until it is tested and tried in the arena of everyday life. One can pretend that things are different, but pretension works only until the testing comes.

Former NBA coach Johnny Kerr said that his biggest test as a coach came when he coached the Chicago Bulls after they first came into the NBA as an expansion team. This was in the "pre-Michael Jordan" days, and the team had lost seven games in a row.

Kerr decided to give the players a pep talk. He told his point guard to go out and pretend that he was the best scorer in the league. He looked at his power forward and told him to go out and pretend that he was the best power forward in the game. He told his team captain to pretend that he was the best offensive rebounder the game had ever seen, and he encouraged his center to pretend that he was the best shot-blocking, rebounding, scoring center who had ever played. Well, to make a long story short, they went out and lost the game by seventeen points.

After the game, the coach was pacing around the locker room, trying to figure out what had gone wrong. The center walked up, put his arm around the coach's shoulder, and told him, "Coach, just pretend we won."

You can pretend for only so long. When the test comes, the real truth will come out. Had Jacob's attitude really changed?

We don't have to wait long to find out if Jacob had really changed, for in the very next episode of Jacob's life, recorded in Genesis 33, we find an account of his next meeting with his estranged brother, Esau. What we witness in this encounter is evidence that Jacob's attitude toward life and in life had indeed been altered. How can we alter our attitudes?

## Learn from Past Mistakes

All of us have made some mistakes. In fact, mistakes are the place where we learn our most profound lessons in life. The only people who haven't made any mistakes are the people who haven't done anything. Therefore, the issue is not whether we make mistakes, but whether we *learn* from our mistakes. Jacob had made some serious mistakes, and his arrogant attitude had made him unteachable up to the point when he wrestled with the angel.

In Genesis 25, when Jacob made the deal with Esau that took away Esau's birthright, Jacob was unfeeling, self-absorbed, and unsympathetic as he watched his brother make a decision that he would regret the rest of his life. Later in Jacob's life, when he had an encounter with God, he was still focused on his own welfare, demanding that God grant him a blessing. During the struggle with God, though, Jacob changed. He had more than met his match. He limped away from the fight, but he was a stronger man from the experience.

After he met with God, Jacob walked out different from the person he had been when he had walked in. He had a different attitude. When he approached Esau, he bowed to the ground. He embraced his brother. He shed genuine tears and referred to himself as Esau's *"servant"* (Gen. 33:5). These are things that the old Jacob would never have done, but he had learned from his mistakes.

Maybe today you see yourself in this story. If so, I say to you: learn from your mistakes. Don't keep going in the direction you've been going. If you've been arrogant in the past, now is the time to alter that attitude. If you have been selfish, deceitful, jealous, or envious, now is the time to alter those attitudes. In the place of arrogance, try thankfulness. Replace selfishness with service. Replace jealousy with joy. Substitute devotion for deceit. Remember, change your attitude, and you change your life.

## Put a Premium on People

All of his life, Jacob had valued possessions over people. Jacob was willing to do anything to get "things." Jacob was willing to hurt whomever he had to and do whatever he had to do just to accumulate things. Yet when Jacob wrestled with the angel, and his name was changed, these were clues that his character was being corrected, and his attitude was about to be altered. He came out of that experience with not only a limp, but also a new outlook. He learned to put a premium on people.

Once Jacob realized this principle, he was then in the position to use his possessions wisely, rather than cling to them selfishly. Look at his attitude later. Flocks and herds were a fragile burden during the long trips through the desert, but Jacob offered to take special care of the flocks and even assume Esau's share of the responsibility.

Before his encounter with God, Jacob would have disregarded Esau's rights. He probably would have found a way to take the entire flock for himself, but his attitude had been altered. He was not the same anymore. He had learned to value people. Do people matter to you? People matter to God. Make that a fundamental value of your spiritual experience: people matter to God.

Because we are related to God through Jesus Christ, people should matter to us. Everything we do should be done to help, teach, uplift, inspire, and empower people. That's our mission in the world. We are called to touch people with love. John 3:16 says, *"God so loved the world* [not the buildings, not the meadows, not the oceans, but the people] *that He gave His only begotten Son, that whoever believes in Him should not perish but have everlasting life."* Previously Jacob had prized his possessions, but presently he put a premium on people.

## Candidly Communicate Your Convictions

Jacob's attitude changed: deceitfulness was replaced by honesty. Jacob had told so many lies to those who cared about him that he probably didn't remember half of them. Some of the lies were "big lies," and few of them were even worth the effort. A deceitful attitude had been a major part of Jacob's character. However, in Genesis 33:10, we cannot help but note how sincere he was about his desire to offer a gift in an effort to mend the relationship with his brother.

Also, in verses 13–14, he was candid with Esau about his disagreement with the way Esau was planning the rest of the journey. Esau wanted them to go forward side by side; Jacob insisted that Esau go on ahead of him. Now, obviously, neither of these was an earth-shattering decision; in fact, each one might even be seen as downright trivial.

Here's the important point: it was a start in the right direction. Jacob was honestly communicating his convictions. For a fellow who had lied so much, so often, for so long, and so unapologetically, *any* display of sincere truthfulness was a major step in the right direction. Lying can grab us in so many different ways.

A story is told about a school principal who received a phone call. The voice said, "Thomas Bradley won't be in school today." The principal was a bit suspicious, so he asked, "And who's speaking?" The voice answered, "This is my father speaking." Here's the point: great big lies might trap one person; another person might get caught in telling a string of "little bitty" lies.

God wants to *alter our attitudes* and set our hearts on the truth. The place to start is with our trivial situations, because that is where deceitfulness and half-truths come to us the easiest. Don't neglect the small stuff. If we get a handle on our attitudes in minor situations, we'll be both equipped and conditioned to cope with the major ones.

## Recognize How Good God Has Been to You

As children, we experience Christmas as a time of getting, of receiving gifts, of asking for "stuff," and so on. As we enter adulthood, gradually the tide begins to turn, so that at some point, Christmas becomes something of an equal balance between getting and giving.

As we get older, perhaps we have children and grandchildren. At that point, Christmas becomes a time of giving more than anything else. The difference is our perspective. As we mature, we stop viewing life as "Christmas through a child's eyes," looking for what we're going to *get*, and we begin to view life as "Christmas through a parent's eyes," looking for what we might have the opportunity to *give*.

This is the attitude alteration we witness in Jacob. He looked at what God had given him, at all the blessings he had, at all the ways that had been made for him, and his heart was prompted to give. He said to Esau, *"God has dealt graciously with me, and…I have enough"* (Gen. 33:11).

No matter what's going on, remember that God has already been good to you. Before his name was changed, Jacob was concerned primarily with *taking*, with getting stuff to be used selfishly. At every opportunity, he took. Yet at the close of this episode in his life, he had finally learned the meaning of *giving*.

In the final moments of this encounter, he offered Esau a *"present"* (v. 10), a present worthy of the years of pain he had caused his brother. When Esau insisted that Jacob keep the gift for himself, Jacob persisted in his request. The old Jacob wouldn't have done that, but the new Jacob desired to give. Jacob said, *"Please, if I have now found favor in your sight, then receive my present from my hand….Please, take my blessing that is brought to you, because God has dealt graciously with me, and because I have enough"* (vv. 10–11). Jacob recognized just how good God had been to him. Do you?

God has already blessed you, lifted you up, made a way for you, and opened doors for you. The Lord woke you up this morning and started you on your way. The Lord walks with you, talks with you, and even whispers in your ear that you are His very own. You are blessed. Today is a wonderful day to do a little *attitude alteration*.

## Prayer:

> Lord, I give You praise for the power to alter my attitudes. I adopt now those attitudes that will bless, uplift, empower, and encourage. I will be candid. I will be honest. I will value people. I recognize just how good You have been to me, and I am grateful. I offer You praise and thanksgiving. Yes, I am glad to be alive! In the name of Christ, Amen.

# 3

# GO FOR THE GOAL

If you want to succeed in life, you must learn how to set goals. Research has revealed that people have more difficulty setting goals than they do accomplishing them once they are set. The hardest part is actually sitting down and thinking about what God wants us to do with our lives. The fact is, many of us have a difficult time planning, but "if you fail to plan, you plan to fail."

A national survey taken a few years ago determined that slightly less than one-third of Americans were living at the level of basic subsistence, a little more than half were just getting by, one-tenth were moderately successful, and only 3 percent could be described as highly successful.

This same survey pointed out that, in terms of attitude, 27 percent had made no effort at all to plan for their future, 60 percent had given some thought to it (they had some vague idea where they were headed, but not much), 10 percent had a good idea where they were headed, but only 3 percent had identifiable, written goals.

Now the interesting thing about this survey was that there was only one major difference between the moderately successful and the highly successful. In every other area—education, talent, resources, skills—they were basically equal. The one difference between the moderately successful and the highly successful was that those who were highly successful had totally definable, written goals. If you want to succeed in life, you have to set goals. If you don't know where you're going, any road will take you there. What does the Bible have to say about goal-setting? Listen. Proverbs 11:27 says, *"He who earnestly seeks good finds favor, but trouble will come to him who seeks evil."* Proverbs 16:9 says, *"We should make plans—counting on God to direct us"* (TLB). Proverbs 24:3–4 says, *"Any enterprise is built by wise planning, becomes strong through common sense, and profits wonderfully by keeping abreast of the facts"* (TLB). What's the point? It's good sense to plan.

It's good sense to establish goals in every area of your life—in your relationships, your family, your job, your business, your finances, and your fitness and nutrition. Also, as a church or as a community of like-minded individuals, we must have goals. Proverbs 13:16 says, *"Every prudent man acts with knowledge, but a fool lays open his folly."* Wise people plan ahead. Wise people set goals.

This is a great time to prayerfully and carefully set goals for every area of our lives, as we seek to maximize our edge in order to face the challenges that lie ahead.

In Genesis 24, there is a ten-step model for effective goal-setting. There, we have the insightful story of Abraham's servant, Eliezer. Abraham had sent him to find a wife for his son Isaac. It is interesting that in this story, in the *New International Version,* the word *success* is used five times. The word *success* is used more in this chapter than in any other place in the Bible, and all the references refer to how to set and reach goals.

The same ten steps that Eliezer used thousands of years ago to accomplish his goal will work for us right now. That's the good news! It doesn't matter whether we're planning a business, a marriage, a career, or a physical fitness program. These ten steps will enable us to effectively go for our goals and attain them. Interested? Get out your highlighter.

## Step #1: Determine Your Position

Ask yourself some questions. Where am I now? What would I like to change? Determine where you are. Evaluate your present condition. Do a frank assessment. Take an honest appraisal of your life. Do a checkup. Frequently, I ask myself, "Lance, where are you headed? Are you heading in the right direction?"

If you were to call me from a phone booth and say, "I want to come over to your house. Give me directions," what would be the first thing I would ask? "Where are you?" I have to know where you are before I can tell you how to get where you want to be.

This truth applies to all of life. Before we can plot a plan to take us where we want to go, we first must know where we are right now. Determine your position. Genesis 24:1 says, *"Now Abraham was old, well advanced in age; and the LORD had blessed Abraham in all things."* Abraham knew God had promised to give him an abundance of

**It's never too late to begin fulfilling your dream.**

descendants. He had a son, a miracle child, but Isaac didn't have a wife yet. So Abraham decided he'd better do something.

I don't care who you are or what your age is, you're never too old to take the steps to fulfill your dream. Although Abraham was about 115 years old, he set a goal to find Isaac a wife.

## Step #2: Define Your Purpose

Plainly state your goal. Define it clearly. Say it out loud. Picture it. Focus on it. Get a specific image in your mind. Know exactly what you want. Put these two things together: know where you are, and know what you want. Abraham said to his servant, *"Go to my country and to my family, and take a wife for my son Isaac"* (Gen. 24:4). Abraham knew exactly what he wanted. His goal was clearly defined. Once Eliezer, Abraham's oldest servant, reached the city of Nahor, he prayed a specific prayer; he asked God to identify the woman who should be Isaac's wife. He prayed,

> *Now let it be that the young woman to whom I say, "Please let down your pitcher that I may drink," and she says, "Drink, and I will also give your camels a drink"; let her be the one You have appointed for Your servant Isaac. And by this I will know that You have shown kindness to my master.*
>
> (Gen. 24:14)

We will never reach vague goals. The more specific a goal is, the easier it is to reach. If you say, "God, bless my life," how will you know when God has blessed your life? Sometimes blessings come disguised as burdens. Sometimes blessings come as storms. What is your goal? You need to be specific. A vague goal has no drawing power. You need to know what you want. Here's a way to get there.

Ask yourself three questions: What do I want to be? That's the *identity* question. What do I want to do? That's the *vocation* question. What do I want to have? That's the *possession* question. You say, "I want to travel." Great. Where? "I want to have income." Good. How much? "I want a career." Fantastic. What kind? "I want to witness." To whom? Be specific. "I want to lose weight." How much? "I want to read the Bible." When? The point is—be specific.

In verse 5, Eliezer had a typical reaction: *"The servant asked him, 'What if* [circle *"what if"* in your Bible] *the woman is unwilling to come back with me to this land?'"* (NIV). The typical reaction whenever you start to set goals is immediately to start to worry. What might go wrong? What if something happens? If you ever want to move from being a "problem haver" to becoming a "problem solver," don't confuse the dreaming phase with the scheming phase. A lot of people don't want to make any decisions until they've solved all their problems in advance. Make the decision; then solve the problem. Don't confuse decision making and problem solving. They are two different aspects.

Let me give you an example. On May 25, 1961, President John F. Kennedy announced to a joint session of Congress, "I believe that this nation should commit itself to achieving the goal, before this decade is out, of landing a man on the moon and returning him safely to the earth."[1] That was the dream. That was the decision. Did he try to figure out all the answers to the problems before he made the decision? No. He set the goal. "We're going to go there." Once the decision making is out of the way, then you move into the problem solving.

**Don't confuse dreaming with scheming.**

When President Kennedy made his statement to Congress, it was physically and technologically impossible to travel to the moon, yet he made the decision and dealt with the obstacles later. Worry and fear can paralyze us. That's why a lot of people don't set goals. They start to set a goal and then say, "What if I don't make it? If I don't make it, then I'll look like a failure." Fear of failure will paralyze you. So what do you do to get rid of the fear and worry?

## Step #3: Discover a Promise

Find a promise you can claim from God's Word, and worry about the *hows* later. Latch on to the promise, and watch God work. In Genesis 24:7, Abraham told his servant about God's promise: *"The LORD...spoke to me and promised me* [circle that] *on oath, saying, 'To your offspring I will give this land'"* (NIV).

This confident attitude is what differentiates a person of faith when he is setting goals. As people of faith, our goal-setting is always to be based on a promise of God. Abraham believed God's promise that he would have offspring—that a great nation would come from his family. He assured his servant of God's faithfulness. He told him, *"He will send His angel before you"* (v. 7).

As a person of faith, when you're setting goals, don't look at your own resources or your own abilities. There are over seven thousand promises in the Bible just waiting to be claimed. They're like blank checks. Let the size of your God determine the size of your goal.

**If God is your Partner, make your plans larger.**

My church family and I have set some very big goals. People say, "Who do you think you are?" I often respond, "That's the wrong question." The issue is not who we think we are, but who we believe God is! Our God is an awesome God! Ask yourself, "What promise can I claim?"

## Step #4: Describe the Profit

Every goal must have a payoff or reward. If there's no reward, then there's no motivation to fulfill it or to reach it. You have to settle the value of the goal in your mind. In Genesis 24:7, Abraham described what would be gained from the trip. He told his servant, *"You shall take a wife for my son from there."*

What motivated Eliezer? Multiple things. Isaac was going to get a wife, God's purpose was going to be fulfilled, Abraham would be pleased, and he himself would be rewarded. There was a payoff to his goal. Ask yourself these five questions:

> What is the reward?
> Why do I want it?
> How will I feel when I get it?
> Why do I want to take this step?
> Why is it important to describe the profit up front?

When you settle the *why*, God will show you the *how*. When you know *why* you want to do what you want to do with your life, you have a calling on your life. You know *why* you are doing what you're doing, and God will show you the *how*. If you don't understand this concept in your life, if you don't know what the profit is, what the payoff is for attaining the goal, or why you're investing your life, then you'll give up when times get tough. You'll become discouraged when things go wrong; then you'll throw in the towel.

In my own life, through prayer, I have identified both the long- and short-term benefits of doing what I do. In the short term—by preaching, teaching, motivating, and writing—I have the incredible joy of knowing that I am fulfilling the purpose for which God gave me life. I was born to preach, to teach, and to motivate people. It is my mission, my focus, and my destiny. I was born to educate, entertain, enlighten, and encourage people.

God has blessed me to have the learning and the burning, the mind and the mouth. As I do what God made me to do, I reap tremendous benefits. In the long term, when that awesome Day comes when I must take off mortality and put on immortality—slip out of time and step into eternity—I want to stand before almighty God and hear Him say, *"Well done, good and faithful servant"* (Matt. 25:21). In that praise-saturated moment, it will be worth everything I had to go through to get there. That's the ultimate payoff.

## Step #5: Desire in Prayer

The Bible says in Mark 11:24, *"Whatever things you ask when you pray, believe that you receive them, and you will have them."* Praying for your goals does two things. First, it reveals desire. It reveals how badly you want something. Often God delays an answer to prayer to see how much we want it, to distinguish if this is a wish or a whim or a deep desire of the heart. It's a sifting process.

If you got everything you ever asked for in prayer, do you realize what a loaded gun prayer would be? None of us would even be here. Thank God that every prayer is not answered in the way we desire. The fact is, God waits to see if we pray about our goals.

Second, not only do our prayers reveal what we desire, but they also show dependence. Whom are you really trusting in to see that this goal is accomplished? If we never pray about a goal, what does that say? It says we don't think we need God's help. We can handle things on our own.

47

Our prayers are clear evidence of how much we're depending on God. Notice what Abraham's servant prayed in Genesis 24:12: *"O LORD God of my master Abraham, please give me success this day, and show kindness to my master Abraham."* Note that word *"success."* Is it ever correct to pray for success? Well, look at the alternative! Are you going to pray, "God, give me failure"?

You do not have to pray for failure. The enemy of our souls is already busy to make sure that some of our efforts are short-circuited. You don't have to pray for failure; it's on the enemy's agenda. Trials and troubles help us to grow, but we do not have to pray for them. They will show up on their own. When you pray for success and about success, when it comes, it will bring glory to God, and it will help other people.

When what we're attempting to accomplish is ultimately for the glory of God and will benefit other people, we don't have to hesitate about asking God to bless it. One of the secrets of this whole story is that Eliezer prayed continuously through this entire process. There are several prayers right in Genesis 24. He prayed before he left for Abraham's homeland. He prayed after he arrived. He prayed in front of Rebekah's family. He constantly bathed his goals in prayer, and that's exactly what we must do.

We should ask ourselves today, Am I praying for my goals, or have I only established them? Your goals shouldn't be the only things on your prayer list, but they definitely should be a part of your prayer list. Lift them up before the Lord and say, "Lord, these are the things I'm trying to accomplish with my life. I want my life to count. I want my life to be worthwhile. I want to make a difference. I want to be significant for Your glory."

**Your goal list should be part of your prayer list.**

## Step #6: Diagnose the Problem

Problems are part of everything in life, so get used to them. Get over it! Take time to identify the roadblocks and obstacles that are in your way, the things that are holding you back. Ask yourself two questions: Why don't I have this already? What are the barriers? There are all types of barriers: emotional, financial, intellectual, relational, and even spiritual.

Think about Eliezer and his search. Talk about serious problems! He had to go to a country he had never been to. He had to find a lady he had never met. He had to convince her to go back and marry a man she had never met. Is this *Mission Impossible* or what? Would you be able to do what he did? Do you think you'd be successful?

Travel to a foreign country, find someone he's never met, bring her back to marry someone she's never met—Abraham's servant had all kinds of problems. He had the problem of finding the right girl. He had the problem of getting the girl's parents to consent. And even after he got their consent, he had to get *her* consent. He had all types of problems, but he didn't run from them.

Look at your problems. Identify them, because in the problems are the seeds of possibility. That leads us to the next step.

## Step #7: Design a Plan

As we look at this story, we see that Eliezer's plan is a masterpiece. It was well thought out. The Bible says,

> *Then the servant took ten of his master's camels and departed, for all his master's goods were in his hand. And he arose and went to Mesopotamia, to the city of Nahor. And he made his camels kneel down outside the city by a well of water at evening time, the time when women go out to draw water. Then he said, "O Lord God of my master Abraham, please give me success this day, and show kindness to my master Abraham."*
> (Gen. 24:10–12)

This was his plan: first, he would take all of the camels and have them kneel down by the water. Then he would ask for a drink of water. If she said, "Let me water your camels, too," he would know that she was the one whom God had chosen. Remember now, the water had to be drawn out by hand, and the average camel can drink up to forty gallons of water. Add up the camels, and we're talking about three hundred gallons of water.

This woman would indeed have to be phenomenal because she would need to draw three hundred gallons by hand: that's my definition of work! The story continues to unfold. The Scripture says,

> *Before he had finished speaking,...Rebekah, who was born to Bethuel, son of Milcah, the wife of Nahor, Abraham's brother, came out with her pitcher on her shoulder. Now the young woman was very beautiful to behold, a virgin; no man had known her. And she went down to the well, filled her pitcher, and came up.* (Gen. 24:15–16)

Remember that the rest of Eliezer's plan was to ask for a drink of water. If she offered him water and then said that she would draw water for his camels, too, she would be God's choice for Isaac. Eliezer had it all laid out. He had a strategic plan.

If we're going to go for the goal, we need to design a plan and plot out a course of action to overcome any problems we have identified. It's not enough just to point out the problems; we have to move to the next step and figure out a way to go around the obstacles. We must plan out a course of action. We need to write down some specific steps and set a deadline for results. We should ask, How do I intend to reach my goal? How long will it take?

## Step #8: Discipline Your Personality

Nothing great is ever accomplished without discipline. The bottom line in our lives is character. While we are working on our goals, God is working on us. God is much more interested in you than in your goals. During the planning, goal-setting, and goal-changing process, God is going to work on you and make changes in you while you are going and growing toward your goal.

Many times when I've spoken to pastors, I've said, "Growing churches require growing pastors." Likewise, growing businesses require growing businesspeople. Growing marriages require growing spouses. Life requires growth. Ask yourself right now, "Where do I need to change?" God is more interested in your person than in your project. What kind of person do you need to become? Eliezer was a key example of personal discipline.

## He Was Disciplined in His Decisions

Genesis 24:21 says, *"And the man, wondering at her, remained silent so as to know whether the LORD had made his journey prosperous or not."* In other words, when he saw this beautiful woman, he wasn't impulsive. He didn't immediately go out and grab her and say, "You're the one!" He was not impulsive in his decision making. He was very thoughtful, methodical, and disciplined.

## He Was Disciplined in His Desire

Genesis 24:33 reads, *"Food was set before him to eat, but he said, 'I will not eat until I have told about my errand.'"* There was a real man. He said, "I'm going to put off personal pleasure until I get the job done." Sometimes you have to delay personal gratification. You have to defer it and put up with inconvenience in order to reach your goal.

Discipline is simply delayed gratification. It's saying, "I'm going to wait. Down the line the results will be greater than if I just go ahead and do what I want to do right now." A disciplined person considers his choices: he can either sit in front of the television and watch it all day, or he can get up and study his Bible. He can start a workout program now or wait until his health fails.

## He Was Disciplined in His Dialogue

Genesis 24:49 states, *"Now if you will deal kindly* [he's talking to the parents of Rebekah] *and truly with my master, tell me. And if not, tell me, that I may turn to the right hand or to the left."* He was very tactful and polite with her parents.

### He Was Disciplined in His Days

To reach any goals in life, you have to learn the art of time management. Ovid once said, "Neither can the wave that has passed by be recalled, nor the hour which has passed return again."

When you're wasting time, you're committing suicide. Your time is your life. Eliezer said, *"Do not hinder me, since the LORD has prospered my way"* (Gen. 24:56). He was careful with how he invested his time. If you want to maximize your edge, you must take control of your time.

## Step #9: Deposit the Price

There is always a price tag for reaching every goal. Great goals require great sacrifices. A lot of people want to reach great goals, but only if it's convenient. Their attitude is, "I have this dream, but I just want to do it in my spare time." Before you pursue your goal, you need to ask yourself three questions: (1) What will it cost me? (2) What am I willing to give? (3) Is it worth it?

Genesis 24:53 says, *"The servant brought out jewelry of silver, jewelry of gold, and clothing, and gave them to Rebekah. He also gave precious things to her brother and to her mother."* Giving is the test of our faith. There's always a price tag in life. No matter what goal you have, there's going to be a cost.

The question you have to ask yourself is, "Is the cause worth the cost? Is it worth my energy? Is it worth my time?" I know some people who have had the goal to build a business, but they lost their families in the process. Was it worth it? No, it was not worth it. Consider the wisdom in this verse, *"What will it profit a man if he gains the whole world, and loses his own soul?"* (Mark 8:36).

## Step #10: Depend on People

We will never achieve very much in life until and unless we learn to get along with other people. John Rockefeller used to say there was one thing he'd pay more for than any other skill, and that was the ability to work with people. Lots of geniuses can't get along with other people. You have to learn to depend on others because God works through people. It takes teamwork and cooperation. Success is never a one-man show. Never. It's always a joint effort.

The secret of a great church is commitment and unity. When there is commitment and cooperation, God can do tremendous things. He can overlook all kinds of other things. Vance Havner said in a sermon, "Snowflakes are frail, but if enough of them stick together they can stop traffic." We may not be able to do a lot individually, but when God's people get together, we can do anything. United we stand. Depend on people.

## Three Cautions in Setting Goals

*First, be flexible.* Be willing to change your plans when they need to be changed. Don't set your goals in concrete. Proverbs 13:19 says, *"It is pleasant to see plans develop. That is why fools refuse to give them up even when they are wrong"* (TLB). Have you ever known people who had a plan, which everybody knew was dying on the vine, but because they had thought it up, they refused to admit its failure? They said, "We may go into the red for another six months, but we're going to stay with this plan." The Bible teaches that wisdom dwells with prudence, knowledge, and discretion (Prov. 8:12). Weigh the risks; evaluate the results. Change your plans when they need to be changed.

*Second, plan for tomorrow, but live in today.* You can't live in yesterday, and you can't live in tomorrow. You can live only in today. Matthew 6:34 says, *"Don't be anxious about tomorrow. God will take care of your tomorrow too. Live one day at a time"* (TLB). You must maintain the fine balance in your life between planning for the future and living for today.

Some people are so future-oriented that all they can think about is tomorrow. They miss today. They don't enjoy it. One of the things God has given me is the ability to truly be where I am: to be all there—to be in the moment! When I'm at a restaurant, I'm all there at the restaurant. I'm not thinking about the church or other things. When I'm at church, I'm all there. It's the ability to really enjoy the moment. You can be so busy planning for the future that you miss out on life. Live one day at a time.

*Third, recognize that God is greater than your plans.* Proverbs 16:1 says, *"We can make our plans, but the final outcome is in God's hands"* (TLB). James 4:13–15 says, *"Come now, you who say, 'Today or tomorrow we will go to such and such a city, spend a year there, buy and sell, and make a profit'; whereas you do not know what will happen tomorrow....Instead you ought to say, 'If the Lord wills, we shall live and do this or that.'"* Go ahead and make plans, but realize that God's purpose is greater than your plans. God has the right at any time to change your plans. Remember, God's ideas are always best.

That's the biblical basis for setting goals. Using these principles will help you to maximize your edge. Use them in all areas of your life. If you're going to go for the goal, remember to do the following: Determine your position. Define your purpose. Discover a promise. Describe the profit. Desire in prayer. Diagnose the problem. Design a plan. Discipline your personality. Deposit the price. Depend on people.

Have you clearly thought out what you want to do with the rest of your life? What do you want written on your tombstone? Begin today to determine what you want to do with your life.

## Prayer:

> Almighty God, I am beginning to see how practical and relevant these words are to my life. Lord, stir up in me a desire to make my life count. I know that "the unexamined life is not worth living."[2] Yet sometimes in the rat race, I'm so busy making a living that I forget to make a life. The Scriptures have taught me to *"ponder the path of* [my] *feet"* (Prov. 4:26) in order to know and discern the direction in which my life is headed. I receive the power now to set significant goals in every area of my life. I pray these things in Jesus' name. Amen.

# 4

# CULTIVATE YOUR CONFIDENCE

Some time ago, a national survey studied the impact of self-esteem and confidence. The results indicated that people with a high level of self-confidence are more successful, more satisfied with their lives, and have more satisfying relationships. They demonstrate a greater willingness to help others in need and are more likely to see God as caring, loving, forgiving, and able. They also tend to be physically healthier, more productive, and less affected by stress. They hold themselves to higher moral and ethical standards and are more likely to assume leadership positions. A sense of self, a sense of your value as a person, and a high level of self-esteem and self-confidence are incredibly important.

## How to Cultivate Your Confidence

In Philippians 1:6, Paul said, *"Being confident of this very thing, that He who has begun a good work in you will complete it until the day of Jesus Christ."* The psalmist said in Psalm 108:1, *"O God, my heart is steadfast."* How do you cultivate that kind of confidence?

### Step #1: Be Yourself

This point may appear to be obvious, but it needs to be reiterated because many people are busy trying to be somebody else. Have you ever noticed how young people want to act and look as if they were older? And older people want to look younger. In today's unisex environment, some women dress like men, and some men dress like women. Those who are pleasingly plump want to be graciously thin, and those who are graciously thin want to be even thinner. Very few people accept themselves as they are.

We watch television and see drop-dead gorgeous women and incredibly handsome hunks. Then we go and look in the mirror. When what we see does not match the image we've seen on television, we become dissatisfied with who we are, discontent with what we are, and disturbed by where we are. We all must learn how to be ourselves.

You're never going to experience any level of confidence or esteem by trying to be somebody else. Have you been to an airport lately? How many people in airports look like people on television? Not very many! The majority of us are just average-looking. Confidence is when you can say as Paul said in 1 Corinthians 15:10, *"By the grace of God I am what I am."* Insecurity is when you're busy trying to be somebody else.

When I first started in ministry, I tried to preach like C. L. Franklin, a popular radio preacher in Detroit, Michigan, in the 1960s and '70s. Later, I wanted to preach like Billy Graham and see thousands of people respond to my messages in the way that people responded to his. Following my love affair with Billy Graham, I wanted to preach like my pastor, Frederick Sampson of the Tabernacle Baptist Church in Detroit, Michigan. I wanted to command audiences with my use of language as I had observed him do on so many occasions. I wanted to be somebody else.

Churches are filled with people trying to be somebody else. They are trying to shout, dance, pray, and talk like someone else. They want to dress like other people, drive what they drive, live where they live, say what they say, and do what they do. They even want to exercise someone else's spiritual gift.

They lack originality and have made themselves content as a copy of someone else. The problem with trying to be somebody else is that you start trying to transform everyone else in your life into someone else. If you are not careful, you will attempt to remake your children into the image of someone else's children, try to make your kids act like their kids, your husband act like someone else's husband, or your wife act like another man's wife. When we are not satisfied with who we are, it makes us dissatisfied with everyone around us. Let me encourage you to *be yourself*.

Romans 12:3 says, *"For I say, through the grace given to me, to everyone who is among you, not to think of himself more highly than he ought to think, but to think soberly, as God has dealt to each one a measure of faith."* Honestly recognize your strengths and your weaknesses; then play to your strengths.

The fact is, we're not all created equal, contrary to the Declaration of Independence. I will never be able to sing like Stevie Wonder, Ray Charles, or Luther Vandross—they're unique. We're not created equal, yet Paul reminded us

> **Focus on your potential, not your limitations.**

in his letter to the church at Rome that God made us just the way we are. God is like a potter with a lump of clay. He makes some of the clay into fine china and some of it into everyday dishes.

The china is not better than the dishes because it gets used only every now and then. The everyday dishes get used all the time. I don't want to be china; make me a coffee cup. I want to be used every day. The china is not better; it's just different. It's God's choice what He makes of you. If you want to cultivate your confidence, be yourself.

## Step #2: Do Your Best

Do your best with what you have. Aim for personal excellence. Your ability is God's gift to you. What you do with it is your gift to God. Galatians 6:4 says, *"Let everyone be sure that he is doing his very best* [circle that], *for then he will have the personal satisfaction of work well done* [circle that], *and won't need to compare himself with someone else"* (TLB).

Paul was trying to teach people to first discover what God made them to be; then, they were to develop what God made them to be. First, discover who you are; then develop who you are. Sometimes we're so busy imitating other people that we don't have time to develop our own talents.

I read a study not long ago that followed 1,500 men and women from age twenty until they were in their forties. Of the 1,500 people, 83 became millionaires. The interesting thing is that none of those who became millionaires set out to be wealthy, while all the other people were involved in get-rich-quick schemes. The secret of those who became millionaires was that each decided very early to specialize in an area of work that he or she loved to do.

**It's more important to do your best than to be the best.**

In specializing, they became so good at their particular skill that they were well paid. The secret is this: specialize until you're special. Do your best. Find what you are good at and work on it. Find your niche, and get better and better and better.

Parents, teach this principle to your kids: not everybody can be the best at everything, but each of us has a gift to do something well. Let your goal be to discover an area where you are gifted, and specialize in it. Get better at it. The verse says that if you do your best, then you won't *"need to compare* [yourself] *with someone else"* (Gal. 6:4 TLB).

## Step #3: Don't Compare

Say this out loud to yourself right now: don't compare. Don't judge yourself by other people. It's difficult to avoid comparing ourselves because we live in an extremely competitive culture. However, in 2 Corinthians 10:12, Paul said to the church at Corinth, *"For we dare not class ourselves or compare ourselves with those who commend themselves. But they, measuring themselves by themselves, and comparing themselves among themselves, are not wise."*

Paul reminded us that every time we compare ourselves with somebody else, it's a bad move; it puts us on an emotional roller coaster. The moment we begin comparing ourselves to somebody else, despite how good we may feel, we go right down the tubes. Don't compare yourself with somebody else.

Ladies, tell the truth. Have you ever gotten all dressed up—you have your makeup on; your lips, hips, and fingertips are looking good; you have that wig or weave laying just right; you're confident in how you look—and then gone to a meeting where "Miss Didn't Work at It, but Still Looks Stunning" walks in? All of a sudden, you can't admit it, but instead of being *the* lady, you start to feel like a *bag* lady. You can always tell when that insecure nerve has been plucked, because it will usually be followed by statements like, "Her dress is all right," or "I would have done something different with my hair," or "That's probably the only nice dress she has." What's the problem? You are comparing yourself to her.

Have you ever gone to class or to a business luncheon and thought to yourself, "I'm intelligent. I'm on top of my job. I'm pretty smart"? Then some hotshot starts spouting million-dollar words you've never heard and computing figures faster than you can envision them. Suddenly, you start to feel like a blubbering idiot. What's the problem? You're comparing yourself to someone else.

The Bible teaches us not to compare ourselves with others. We all have a radar dish with which we are constantly scanning and comparing ourselves with everybody else. As kids, when we were being given dessert, we couldn't even enjoy it because of looking around to see who may have gotten a little bit more than we did. As students, we compared test grades and prom dates. As adults, we compare lawns, homes, cars, clothes, and jewelry. Don't compare!

In Psalm 73:2–3, the psalmist said, *"But as for me, my feet had almost stumbled; my steps had nearly slipped. For I was envious of the boastful, when I saw the prosperity of the wicked."* No habit is as destructive to your self-esteem and self-confidence as comparing yourself with someone else. Every time we compare, we're damaging our emotions. These are self-inflicted scars. When we compare ourselves to other people, the result of that comparison is always vanity or bitterness. Always.

We can always find somebody whose work is inferior to our work, and that discovery fills us with foolish pride. We think, "I'm pretty good!" In addition, we can always find somebody who's doing a better job than we are, and that can make us bitter, jealous, and discouraged. Either way, whenever we compare, we end up with the short end of the stick. Don't compare, because you are utterly unique.

Nobody has been through what you've been through. Nobody knows the trouble you've seen. Nobody completely understands what you had to come through to get where you are today. Nobody has had to bear your burdens. Cry your tears. Carry your cross. Fight your battles. Suffer your setbacks. Walk your road. Endure your heartaches. Struggle at midnight. Nobody knows like you know what the Lord has done for you. You are unique. Nothing and nobody compares to you. Comparisons are irrelevant. Don't ever compare yourself; it's completely pointless.

**You are in a class all by yourself.**

When we compare, it's analogous to saying, "I can bench-press more than my grandmother." So what? It's like comparing submarines to tangerines: it doesn't quite fit. Human beings are unique; we're not the same. We're all different. If you want to cultivate your confidence, be yourself, do your best, and don't compare.

## Pick Positive Friends

Self-esteem and self-confidence are primarily influenced by our relationships, so we need to select our friends very carefully; this is critical. The company you keep will have a dramatic effect on your self-esteem and self-confidence. First Corinthians 15:33 says, *"Bad company corrupts good character"* (NIV). Parents, we teach our kids this principle repeatedly: birds of a feather flock together.

If you want to soar with the eagles, you can't run with the turkeys. You have to select your friends wisely. They have a big influence on your life. If you want to be confident, you have to associate with and surround yourself with confident, godly people. Pick positive friends.

A lot of people get what I call the Charlie Brown syndrome. Charlie Brown is the world's greatest loser. He never does anything right. There's no doubt in my mind why he's such a loser. It's Lucy! No doubt about it! Lucy is always telling Charlie Brown what is wrong with him, why his ideas are dumb. In one instance, she lambastes him with eight demoralizing zingers in a row. She doesn't even stop for a breath. With friends like Lucy, who needs enemies?

Tragically, many people have toxic friends who are systematically damaging their self-esteem through insults, put-downs, irritation, degradation, and criticism. Some people believe it's their mission in life to put you down. I tell people all the time, "You don't have to put yourself down; I know plenty of people who will do it for you."

How do you handle negative people? You can't change them. That's not your job; that's God's job. You can change only yourself—by the grace of God, through the Spirit of God, with help from the Word of God. So what do you do with negative people? You limit your exposure to them as much as possible. *"Blessed is the man who walks not in the counsel of the ungodly,...nor sits in the seat of the scornful"* (Ps. 1:1). Proverbs 11:9 teaches us, *"With his mouth the godless destroys his neighbor"* (NIV). Limit your exposure.

Some of you need to change jobs. Some of you need to end your relationship with a boyfriend or a girlfriend who says he or she loves you, but then treats you like dirt. Love is not supposed to hurt. You say, "I can't leave. It's my family."

If you're in a situation like that, let me say two things: first, if you are using put-downs and constant criticism to try to shape your family members, God wants me to tell you, "Knock it off!" You're systematically destroying your family. Don't do it.

Second, if you are on the receiving end of somebody's knife of criticism and your heart and spirit are constantly being cut, you need a support group. You need to surround yourself with positive people who will work through prayer, Bible study, fellowship, and encouragement to build you up, because their actions will counteract those from people who are busy working to put you down. Pick positive friends. Am I helping you? Read on.

## Invest Your Life

The most confident people I know are those who have a sense of purpose for living. They know where they're going. If you want to be confident, invest your life in a cause greater than yourself— something that draws you outside of yourself. Your self-confidence will soar. It will give you a reason to get out of bed in the morning. Make something of your life.

Matthew 16:25–26 says, *"For whoever desires to save his life will lose it, but whoever loses his life for My sake will find it. For what profit is it to a man if he gains the whole world, and loses his own soul?"* This is Jesus talking. He's saying that we discover ourselves when we give ourselves away. Self-confidence is definitely not self-centeredness. There's a difference.

Self-centeredness leads to insecurity. It's not by accident that the "Me Generation" is the most insecure generation that our nation has produced. You need to be self-confident without being self-centered. How do you do that? You give your life away to a great cause, a great purpose.

Golda Meir, the former prime minister of Israel, said that as a child she was disturbed by her lack of physical beauty. She said that as she grew older, she overcame her feelings of inferiority by discovering what she wanted to do with her life. Then her physical appearance lost its significance. She said, "Not being beautiful was the true blessing....Not being beautiful forced me to develop my inner resources."[1]

There's a big myth that successful people don't have weaknesses. That's not true. Successful people have as many or more weaknesses than unsuccessful people do. It's just that they don't let it bother them. They go on with their lives. They find out the weaknesses that they can change or improve, and they work on those. Then they do their best and forget the rest.

In a study compiled in their book *Cradles of Eminence*, Victor Goertzel and Mildred George Goertzel researched the family backgrounds of over four hundred "eminent" people of the first half of the twentieth century. The individuals studied had made notable contributions or had brought about significant change in society—for good or evil. The authors discovered that 75 percent of these influential people were troubled as children either by poverty, broken homes, or parents who rejected or dominated them.

Twenty-five percent of those studied had some type of physical handicap. How did the children who experienced these handicaps manage to become eminent in spite of their difficult and deprived backgrounds? The study reported that many of these individuals identified the need to compensate for such handicaps as a determining factor in their drive for achievement.[2]

We may conclude that those who overcame adversity as children and became prominent as adults did so by compensating for their weaknesses, by specializing in areas that they loved or excelled in, and by becoming successful at what they chose to do. Rather than dwelling on what they couldn't do, they focused on what they could do, and they made something of their lives. They had purpose.

The world stands aside for the person—man or woman—who knows where he or she is going. Lose your life to find it. Give it away. Focus your life. Some of you say, "Lance, I'm just too old. I've missed my chance."

At 53, Margaret Thatcher became the first female prime minister of Great Britain. At 64, Francis Chichester sailed around the world by himself in a fifty-three-foot yacht. At 72, Golda Meir became the prime minister of Israel. At 75, Ed Delano of California bicycled 3,100 miles in thirty-three days to attend a fiftieth college reunion in Massachusetts. At 73, Grandma Moses decided to start painting. She gave her first exhibition at age 80. At 81, Ben Franklin served as a mediator between opposing factions at the U.S. Constitutional Convention. At 96, George Selbach scored a 110-yard hole in one in Indian River, Michigan. That's a long shot for a 96-year-old! On his one hundredth birthday, ragtime pianist Eubie Blake explained, "If I'd known I was going to live this long, I'd have taken better care of myself." It's never too late.[3]

If you want to be a confident person, be yourself. Don't try to be anybody else. You can't be anyone else even if you try. God wants you to be you. He made you to be you. Be yourself. Don't focus on the things you can't do. Improve what you can improve. God doesn't expect you to be good in everything. Do your best, and forget the rest.

Every time you compare yourself, you're damaging your uniqueness. You're destroying yourself and putting yourself down. Pick positive friends. Associate with people who build you up and who don't tear you down. Limit your exposure to negative people who are always putting you down.

If there are some critical, negative people from whom you can't get away, counteract their influence by joining a positive support group that will give you authentic, loving care and build you up in the name of the Lord. Invest your life. Don't waste it, and don't spend it. Invest your life in a cause that is greater than yourself.

## Trust God Always

Jeremiah 17:7 says,

> *Blessed is the man who trusts in the Lord and has made the Lord his hope and confidence. He is like a tree planted along a riverbank, with its roots reaching deep into the water—a tree not bothered by the heat nor worried by long months of drought. Its leaves stay green, and it goes on producing all its luscious fruit.* (TLB)

Life can be difficult; life can be tough. The metaphor in this text mentions two types of difficulty: *"heat"* and *"drought."* Heat represents those things in life of which we all have need, but of which we don't want too much. Even good things become bad things when we get too much of them. For example, going to church is good, but if you go to church all day long, seven days a week, your life is going to be out of balance, your boss is going to fire you, and you'll probably be evicted.

Eating "soul food" is a good thing. I'm on a health program, but every now and then, I need a thick slice of pound cake and a healthy slice of sweet potato pie. As long as I indulge only periodically, this need is justifiable and livable. However, if I indulged in these delicacies every day, it would become problematic.

Exercise is a good thing. However, if you work out all day, every day, then your muscles cannot recuperate and heal, and the tissues start to break down. When you get to spend some of the money you make, that's a good thing; but if you start spending and can't stop yourself, you are headed for financial disaster.

In the above text, heat represents those things in our lives that we need but must regulate and balance, and drought represents extremity. Drought is a period of long-lasting heat during which moisture is scant. Note the movement of the text from describing a condition in which we have what we need and are balanced, to depicting a state in which we have too much of something and now need what is not available: that is drought.

Drought represents those places in our life experiences where, for long periods, we must go without something we feel we need. It refers to periods when we are compelled to go without work, income, energy, or perhaps companionship. How are we to handle it when the heat is on and will not go away?

Notice three words that appear in Jeremiah 17:7: *"trusts," "hope,"* and *"confidence."* The writer said, *"Blessed is the man who trusts in the Lord and has made the Lord his hope and confidence."* He was talking about a relationship with God.

When you trust in God, you have a relationship with Him. These challenges will not overwhelm you because, while you appreciate the heat, you're not dependent on it. Even in the middle of an extended drought, the person who trusts in the Lord still has a source of vitality. It's hidden, out of sight, unseen, yet for the person of faith, there are roots. The person who trusts God is rooted in Him and can still be fruitful, even when everybody else is rotting on the vine.

When you are rooted in a relationship with God and have confidence in the Lord, it makes a difference. We've got a lot of tumbleweed Christians today. When the heat comes, they dry up and blow away because they have no roots. When times get tough and the road gets rough, they forget their faith and their church. They forget God because their trust is in something else.

To them, God is an afterthought—an item added to their schedule. Jesus is added to their repertoire for good measure—just to ensure that all the bases are covered. Christ is not the root of their lives, the foundation, the source of their confidence. He is just an addendum.

What is the source of your confidence? Some of you are trusting in your careers. You've got it made. You're on the fast track, and things are going great. When you're hot, you're hot! Some of you are trusting in your bank account. Some of you are trusting in your good looks. Some of you are trusting in your spouses or your parents; they are the rock of stability in your life.

All those things are good, but there's one problem. Every one of those things can be taken away from you. You can lose your career, your money, your health, your spouse, and your family. Then what will you do?

To have ultimate confidence, you must put your confidence in something that can never, ever be taken from you: your relationship to God through Jesus Christ. Don't trust in or base your confidence on people, or on what they say or don't say about you.

Don't place your confidence in your bank account. Don't place it in your spouse. Although you love your spouse, one of you is likely to die before the other. Then where will you be? Trust God always. Then when the heat is on and the drought comes, you won't wither away, because your roots will be so deep that you'll keep on producing no matter what.

How do I trust in God? Look at what Jesus said, *"Whoever hears these sayings of Mine, and does them, I will liken him to a wise man who built his house on the rock"* (Matt. 7:24). You study the Bible, memorize Scripture, read Scripture, and practice Scripture. Build the house of your life on a solid foundation. Then when the winds come and the rains fall, you will stand firm.

**Cultivate your confidence by trusting in God alone.**

## Prayer:

> God, I've trusted in a lot of other things, including myself, but now I want to learn to trust solely in You. I want You in my life. Help me to be myself. Help me to do my best and not worry about the rest. Help me not to compare myself with others. Help me to choose positive friends. Help me to invest my life in something that is greater than myself. God, help me always to trust You and to put my hope in You. That's my prayer, Lord. In Jesus' name, Amen.

# 5

# CONQUER YOUR CIRCUMSTANCES

Things don't always go as planned. Many circumstances we encounter in life appear to be absolutely uncontrollable. Businesses go bankrupt, employees get fired, students get passed over for scholarships, plans fail, friends move away, and athletes lose games.

Life doesn't always go the way we want it to go. One of the inevitable facts of life is that sooner or later we will find ourselves in circumstances over which we have no control.

For instance, we didn't choose who our parents would be. We didn't choose our races or our genders. We didn't choose when and where we would be born or the circumstances surrounding our births. All of these things are the cards that we have been dealt in life.

But how we play them, the hand we make of them, is our choice. As Kenny Rogers sang, "You've got to know when to hold 'em, know when to fold 'em, know when to walk away, and know when to run." And if you don't know, you'd better ask somebody.

Our lives are littered with circumstances we cannot control; however, the message in this chapter is not about controlling circumstances, but about conquering them. To control circumstances implies that you can guide, direct, and manipulate things, but to conquer means that you prevail, succeed, annex, achieve, acquire, take over, obtain, and overcome. You win despite the circumstances. And while we cannot control what happens around us or to us, we can always manage what happens in us.

If you can handle yourself, if you can hold on to yourself, if you can just keep the faith, if you cling to your hope, if you endure the night, if you can walk through the valley of the shadow of death, if you weather the storm, if you brave the hardship, if you can just hold out until tomorrow, everything will be all right. And that's where we want to focus: not on how to control your circumstances, but on how to conquer them.

We can learn this lesson from the testimony of a man named Joseph. Joseph was not given an ideal set of circumstances in life, but because of his inner resources, he was able to persevere, hold on, keep his chin up, continue hopeful, remain consistent, and trust God to work things out in due season. His life was peppered with adversity and hardship. We've all known people who have had to overcome great adversity and incredible hardships in order to live happy lives.

Happiness is not found in the absence of struggle, conflict, and pain, but happiness is discovered in the determination to stay with the struggle, work through the conflict, bear the pain, and come out on the other side someway, somehow.

## From Prisoner to Prince

In Genesis 37–50, we find the story of Joseph. His story has it all—revenge, deceit, lust, attempted seduction, violence, accusations of rape, false charges, and imprisonment. Joseph's life would make a great television miniseries. Joseph was able to rise from the pit of misfortune to the palace of privilege. God blessed him, and he rose from being a prisoner in the jail to being a prince in the house of Pharaoh. Don't tell me what God cannot do!

Egypt was the most powerful nation on the planet at that time, yet God blessed Joseph, an Israelite. God is able—if you trust Him, lean on Him, and wait on Him—to lift you up. Joseph's life was a stunning success story. He shows us that what really counts in life is not your circumstances, but your character.

> **Your character, not your circumstances, will determine what you do with your life.**

Are you familiar with chaotic circumstances? I mean where you're in a situation that's just plain raggedy: nothing's going right, and nobody's acting right. There's no sense of order, propriety, protocol, or structure. Things are just plain chaotic. Joseph was in a chaotic situation. His difficulties could be summarized in three words: *rejected, slandered,* and *forgotten.*

He was *rejected* at home. His half brothers didn't like him and were jealous of him. That's a bad circumstance. The wife of his boss tried to seduce him, then *slandered* him. When he refused to submit to Potiphar's wife's sexual invitations, she told lies to his boss that cost him his job. He was *forgotten* by so-called friends. As long as he was helping them, they were best buddies, but when he needed a hand—when he needed a good word put in for him—they completely forgot him.

The first thirty years of his life, many things didn't go right. He was the second to last of twelve brothers. There was a lot of rivalry and competition and bitterness. The Bible says that the half brothers of Joseph were jealous of him. There was preferential treatment in the household. Joseph came from a difficult environment, a dysfunctional family.

His older brothers didn't like him. In fact, the text testifies that his brothers hated him so much they wouldn't even speak to him in a friendly manner. One day, as they saw him approaching in the field, they said, *"Let us now kill him and cast him into some pit; and we shall say, 'Some wild beast has devoured him'"* (Gen. 37:20). Now,

71

if that's being loved, we don't need to be hated. They threw him into a well, and soon some slave merchants came by. At the suggestion of his brother Judah, they sold him *for twenty shekels of silver"* (v. 28). Chaotic circumstances. Can you see it?

Joseph was taken to Egypt, and there he was sold to a man named Potiphar. He became Potiphar's slave. Almost overnight, he went from being a pampered son to being a subdued slave. His family had rejected him. Rejection hurts. Joseph knew rejection. Yet, in the employment of Potiphar, he became very successful. He didn't permit the weight of his luggage to hinder his trip. He went on anyhow. He was put in charge of everything in Potiphar's home. But Potiphar's wife got eyes for Joseph because Scripture tells us, *"Joseph was well-built and handsome"* (Gen. 39:6 NIV).

Potiphar's wife tried to seduce him. The Bible says,

> *It came to pass after these things that his master's wife cast longing eyes on Joseph, and she said, "Lie with me.". . .So it was, as she spoke to Joseph day by day, that he did not heed her, to lie with her or to be with her.* (Gen. 39:7, 10)

Not once, not twice, but every day, it was the same thing. Sexual harassment in the workplace is at least four thousand years old. And as quiet as it's kept, it works both ways: men to women and women to men. Joseph refused to submit to her advances. He held on to his morals.

Potiphar's wife, however, refused to be dissuaded. At one point, in a fit of passion, she grabbed Joseph by the robe, but he slipped out of it. He lost his coat but kept his character. Yet then, she framed him. As William Congreve said, "Heaven has no rage like love to hatred turned / Nor hell a fury like a woman scorned."[1] When "Big Daddy Potiphar" came home, his wife had her tears flowing, her mascara running, and all her sobs timed just right. She lied about Joseph. First, she told her servants:

> *"Look," she said to them, "this Hebrew has been brought to us to make sport of us! He came in here to sleep with me, but I*

*screamed. When he heard me scream for help, he left his cloak beside me and ran out of the house." She kept his cloak beside her until his master came home.* (Gen. 39:14–16 NIV)

Then she told her husband the story. She said, *"That Hebrew slave you brought us came to me to make sport of me. But as soon as I screamed for help, he left his cloak beside me and ran out of the house"* (vv. 17–18). Joseph was slandered at work. As a consequence, he was thrown into prison for a crime he didn't commit. He was falsely accused. Things went from bad to worse. Once he was in prison, his friends forgot him. This is what happened: in prison, he befriended two of Pharaoh's staff—his butler and his baker. After interpreting a dream for the butler, or cupbearer, Joseph told him, *"Remember me when it is well with you, and please show kindness to me; make mention of me to Pharaoh, and get me out of this house"* (Gen. 40:14). Joseph had helped Pharaoh's chief butler out, but once the butler was released, he promptly forgot about Joseph. The cupbearer didn't give Joseph another thought; he forgot all about him for two whole years.

Sometimes jealous people will try to hurt you, immoral people will try to tempt you, and ambitious people will try to use you; but remember, if you have God in the center of your life, you can conquer the most chaotic set of circumstances. It does not matter whether we speak of trouble at home, hardship at work, or challenges in our relationships: God can teach us how to work things out. This text testifies that despite the chaotic circumstances that surrounded Joseph, *"The LORD was with Joseph, and he was a successful man"* (Gen. 39:2).

In Joseph's story, we unearth a clue that instructs us *not* to curse the chaos that surrounds us, because although we may not see it, the chaos is pregnant with possibility. Let me explain. Genesis 1:1–2 says, *"When God began creating the heavens and the earth, the earth was a shapeless, chaotic mass, with the Spirit of God brooding over the dark vapors"* (TLB). God is in your chaos.

It was into chaos that God stepped. It was *into* chaos that God spoke, and it was *out of* chaos that He created the cosmos. A chaotic situation is pregnant with potential; it requires only someone with enough inner power to deliver the child. Right now, no matter what your chaotic circumstances may be, there's potential there. You cannot always see the potential in your chaos. It may not be apparent to you, but it's there.

Inside that mountain you face is a gold mine. Within your struggle

**Recognize the potential in your chaos.**

is unseen strength. Buried deep in your problems is possibility. Behind your dark cloud is a silver lining. Tap into the inner strength of your soul, the power of your mind, the force of your will, and the anointing of almighty God.

## The Value of Consistent Character

Whenever you are faced with chaotic circumstances, remember that God can work in the circumstances and through the circumstances to craft your character, strengthen your spirit, clarify your convictions, and fortify your faith. Joseph's character was consistent. That's the key to conquering your circumstances: character.

More than once, we read these words: *"The LORD was with Joseph."* (See Genesis 39:2, 21, 23.) One plus God equals a majority. Why was God with Joseph? Because of his character. You may ask, What was the content of his character that made him so incomparable? What should I do when circumstances seem to work against me and my dream? What do I do to make my life count? How can I make an impact when it seems like everything is conspiring to make me mediocre?

Do three things: First, *fulfill your responsibilities.* Wherever you are, do what God has called you to do right there. Next, *maintain your integrity.* No matter what happens in the situation, keep your purity and integrity, and maintain your standard. Third, *trust God's sovereignty.* Believe that God is in control no matter what happens.

74

I heard A. Louis Patterson of the Mount Corinth Church in Texas say, "God can change anything, conquer anything, or control anything. If God does not conquer it, change it, or control it, then we are to continue celebrating in our circumstances and wait to see what the end will be." That's how you conquer your circumstances. That's how you pull success out of failure. Fulfill your responsibilities, maintain your integrity, and trust God's sovereignty.

Joseph was dependable and reliable. He always gave his best—no matter what. As a result, he was promoted to leadership. Genesis 39:6 says that Potiphar had *"left in Joseph's care everything he had* [underline that]; *with Joseph in charge, he did not concern himself with anything except the food he ate"* (NIV). Joseph made every decision in Potiphar's household except what Potiphar would eat.

Potiphar had no worries. Can your boss say that about you? The Bible says Potiphar prospered because of Joseph. Does your boss prosper because of you? Does your family prosper because of you? Wherever Joseph went, he was a blessing, and that must be our goal as people of faith. Be a blessing wherever you go.

**Be a blessing wherever you go.**

When Joseph was unjustly incarcerated, the Scriptures report,

> *The keeper of the prison committed to Joseph's hand all the prisoners who were in the prison; whatever they did there, it was his doing. The keeper of the prison did not look into anything that was under Joseph's authority, because the LORD was with him; and whatever he did, the LORD made it prosper.*
> (Gen. 39:22–23)

Isn't that strange—to put a prisoner in charge of prison affairs? However, after Joseph assumed administrative responsibility, the prison officials had no more worries, because Joseph took care of everything. Joseph was an absolutely incredible brother! You can't keep a good man down! He gets thrown into prison, and the next thing, he's the assistant warden! The cream rises to the top.

If life gave Joseph a lemon, he made lemonade. His response to life's misfortunes was: "I don't know why these things are happening to me, but I do know how I'm supposed to act. I don't know why these circumstances have occurred in my life, but I do know who is Lord of my life." The Scriptures tell us that whenever people turned any responsibility over to Joseph, they didn't have to worry at all; Joseph was reliable.

Can I encourage you today? Let the works you do speak for you.

> **Some people dream of what could happen; others wake up and make things happen.**

Do you do your best with your job, on your job, at your job—even if you hate your job? Why should you always try to do your best? Because ultimately, God is your Source. You represent God. Joseph was in prison on false charges, yet he rose to the top. Don't spend all your time dreaming about what "might be" or the things you'd like to see. Do your best.

Eventually Joseph got promoted. Pharaoh said, "Who could do a better job than Joseph? For he is a man who is obviously filled with the Spirit of God." (See Genesis 41:38.) There is no record that Joseph was always talking about God, or claiming to be filled with the Spirit of God, yet even Pharaoh had to acknowledge what was obvious. Joseph was filled with the Spirit of God. The Holy Spirit was evident in Joseph's life. Can Christ be seen in your life?

There's a direct correlation between shoddy workmanship and a poor testimony. When I call myself a child of God and I don't do good work, that's an insult to God's reputation. It doesn't insult God's character because nobody can touch God's character, but it can damage God's reputation. A believer should be known for excellence, for integrity, for honesty, and for kindness. If you're truly a believer, you ought to do your job to the best of your ability and relate well with the people with whom you work.

Whatever comes up doesn't come out when God is in your heart. In other words, the Spirit controls your actions. You may be tempted to respond in anger, but the Spirit helps you to react in the way that you should.

Perhaps that's the problem: we're not filled; our spiritual tanks are just about empty. When your tank is low, that's not an indictment; it's an indication that you need to pull in and fill up. There's nothing wrong with your motor. You don't need a new car. You just need to fill up. When Pharaoh needed someone to prepare his country for the famine that Joseph told him was coming, Pharaoh said to his servants, *"Can we find such a one as this, a man in whom is the Spirit of God?"* (Gen. 41:38).

Our goal should be to do our personal best at work no matter what our work is—shining shoes, flipping burgers, inputting data, dispensing medication, working in ministry, teaching students, arguing cases, servicing clients, whatever. We're not called to be better than other people, but we are called to be the best we can be. I'm not called to be the best pastor in America; I am called to be the best pastor I can possibly be. You're called to be the best that you can be.

> **The quality of your work reveals the quality of your spiritual life.**

Joseph succeeded and ended up second in command, despite his circumstances or environment, because wherever he was, no matter where he was serving, he gave it his best shot. It didn't matter who his boss was. The issue is not who your boss is; the issue is who you are.

## Fulfill Your Responsibility

Let me share this little law of success. Are you ready for it? Luke 16:10 says, *"He who is faithful in what is least is faithful also in much; and he who is unjust in what is least is unjust also in much."* From time to time, you'll hear people say, "When I make it big, *then* I'm going to be faithful!" But the real question is, "What are you doing about the day-to-day responsibilities you have right now?" Are you being faithful in the little things?

"Man, just as soon as I get out of debt, I'm going to start tithing." Whom are you kidding? "When everything gets settled down, I'll start reading my Bible." If you're not faithful with little responsibilities, why should God bless you with great responsibilities. If you're not faithful with a little amount of money, why should God bless you with a great amount of money.

You need to fulfill your responsibility; in whatever you're doing, do the best you can. No matter what you are doing, you have the opportunity to develop and demonstrate faithfulness. In everything you do, people are watching you, and God is watching you. Are you being faithful in the little things?

Colossians 3:23–24 says, *"Whatever you do, do it heartily, as to the Lord and not to men, knowing that from the Lord you will receive the reward of the inheritance; for you serve the Lord Christ."* God always rewards faithfulness in the little things. Are you waiting for that big break? Know what to do in the meantime? Be faithful in the little things. How do you conquer your circumstances? Fulfill your responsibility right now—your responsibility to your family, your church, your boss, your nation, and your God.

## Maintain Your Integrity

Joseph was a man of moral purity. He was so spotless that people had to fabricate lies about him. My prayer for each of us is that we will live in such a way that people will have to concoct lies in order to accuse and attack us. In Genesis 39:10, we read that Potiphar's wife came to Joseph on a daily basis, trying to seduce him, but Joseph *"did not heed her, to lie with her or to be with her."*

Can you imagine the internal battle going on in this guy's head? He refused to give in. He could have rationalized: "I'm a slave against my will in a foreign country. Life has not gone as I've planned it. I've lost my dream; I might as well lose my morals, too! Life is tough! I owe it to myself to get a little pleasure. Who cares? What's God done for me? My life is going in reverse. I'm not upwardly mobile; I'm in a downward spiral. Besides, if I befriend the boss's wife, I might even get more promotion." Despite any inner struggles he might have had, Joseph would not give in.

How could Joseph maintain his standard of purity and moral integrity even when his world was falling apart? What motivated him? The Bible reveals two answers: his loyalty to others and his love for God. He said, *"My master...has committed all that he has to my hand....How then can I do this great wickedness, and sin against God?"* (Gen. 39:8–9). Whenever we sin, we hurt somebody else. Whenever we lower our integrity, we hurt other people. Joseph said, "I'm not going to do it! It would be a sin against God." And he would not give in!

Proverbs 14:32 says, *"When calamity comes, the wicked are brought down, but even in death the righteous have a refuge"* (NIV). The newspaper proves this point every day. We reap what we sow. If you want to know about the foolishness of immorality, read Proverbs. Whenever you lower any area of your integrity, you damage yourself and somebody else.

When you resist temptation, you're not going to feel good about it all the time. But you don't do right because it feels good; you do right because it is good. I imagine that Joseph was probably saying to himself, when he kept turning down Potiphar's wife, "I've got to be crazy to walk away from this! Nobody would know."

Some of you might think, "If I could make one little change on this income tax form and fill in the wrong figure, I could save megabucks! I must be crazy not to do it—to fudge a little bit here and save myself this money. No one will ever know. I'll conveniently forget to tell the whole story. I'll just shave the truth a little bit." But whether it feels good or not, do what's right. Resist temptation.

Songwriter Horatio R. Palmer said it well:

> Yield not to temptation,
> For yielding is sin.

79

Each vict'ry will help you
Some other to win.

Ask the Savior to help you,
Comfort, strengthen, and keep you.
He is willing to aid you;
He will carry you through.[2]

In the long run, it always pays to do the right thing—always.

Joseph's integrity prevailed. He said, "No!" and he got fired from his job and thrown into jail. Potiphar's wife grabbed him and took his coat. He left his coat, but he kept his character. I can't tell you how many people I know who gave up their morals because their marriages were falling apart, their jobs were on the skids, or their children were giving them trouble.

I challenge you to stay pure. You will save yourself so many heartaches, and you'll have God's blessing on your life. Nothing can take the place of that! When circumstances are chaotic and things aren't working out right, fulfill your responsibility and maintain your integrity.

## Trust God's Sovereignty

God has it all under control. When Joseph was still a young man, God gave him a dream of making an impact with his life. One day in total naïveté, he shared the dream with his brothers and father. He told them, "God gave me this dream that one day everyone is going to bow down to me, even you guys. Isn't that great?" How would you like your younger brother to say that to you? They weren't too excited. Joseph's dream was true, but it was very unwise for him to share it with his family.

For thirty years, Joseph's life went downhill. During that entire time, God never explained to him what was going on, and Joseph had no idea why things were happening as they were. He had every reason to doubt God's love. He could have said, "God, You gave me a dream. What happened?" He had every reason to be bitter. He could have asked, "Why me, God? You gave me a dream, and now I end up a slave, falsely accused of rape, and in prison in a foreign country." But without answers, he continued to trust in God, and that's what faith is all about.

Dr. Frederick G. Sampson said, "Faith is that awesome power that enables a person to resist the terrible necessity of scaling down their dreams, hopes, and aspirations to the level of the event that is their immediate circumstance."[3] Joseph didn't have answers, but he kept on, and years later it all became clear. The Bible tells us that Joseph was eventually promoted to be second in command under Pharaoh, after he interpreted Pharaoh's dream.

I can hear Joseph telling Pharaoh, "We're going to have seven years of plenty, then seven years of famine." Pharaoh asked, "What should we do?" and Joseph answered, "We ought to start a national savings system where for seven years we save all the extra crops and put them in storage. Then when the seven years of famine come, Egypt will have plenty to eat." Pharaoh responded by saying to Joseph, "You're in charge! You do it!" And Joseph did.

God blessed Joseph so much that when the seven years of famine came, Egypt not only had more than enough food, but also enough to sell to other nations. Many came to Egypt to buy food, and among them were his brothers. Years later, long after they had attempted to murder him, long after they had sold him into slavery, Joseph's own brothers came to Egypt to buy food. Joseph's brothers did not recognize him. What would you do in that face-to-face encounter? He's second in command. He could have had them taken away! He could have ordered their execution immediately, but he didn't.

In Genesis 45:7–8, Joseph told his brothers, *"God sent me before you to preserve a posterity for you in the earth, and to save your lives by a great deliverance. So now it was not you who sent me here, but God."* Here are two very important lessons to learn if you're going to successfully navigate life's challenges:

First, realize that *pain often has a hidden purpose.* Usually you don't figure out what the purpose is until after the pain is over. We rarely see the purpose of pain while we are still suffering.

Second, understand that *pain redirects our pilgrimage.* God often redirects our lives through failures, mistakes, disappointments, and brokenness. God can use these experiences to channel our lives into the path He wants us to travel.

Joseph said, *"God sent me before you"* (Gen. 45:7). Notice his reaction to his brothers who had tried to murder him. Genesis 50:20 reports that Joseph said, *"You meant evil against me; but God meant it for good, in order to bring it about as it is this day, to save many people."* All of us have been hurt by somebody in the past, but God can take that hurt and make it work for our good.

**God has a plan that is greater than your problem.**

One of the most popular words today is the word *victim.* It seems that we're all victimized now. In Christ, though, you don't have to stay a victim. You can be a victor! But you have to trust God's sovereignty. If you don't, hurt will make you bitter. God has your best interests at heart. He is in control. He knows just how much you can bear.

Joseph had a persistent faith. He waited years for his dream to come true. For thirty years, nothing went right. Even when he didn't understand his circumstances, Joseph trusted God. Where did his dreams get him? Into slavery. Where did his integrity get him? Into prison. Where did his helping others get him? Nowhere. Yet you don't see him bathing in bitterness or having a pity party.

You see him fulfilling his responsibility, doing the best he could with what he had, and doing the very best wherever he was. You see him maintaining his integrity. He might have lost his dream, but he was not going to lose his morals. You see him trusting God's sovereignty. He believed that God had a plan for his life.

What do you do when circumstances dispute the dream God has given you? You do what Proverbs 3:5–6 says, *"Trust in the LORD with all your heart, and lean not on your own understanding.* [Don't try to figure it all out. Trust in God, and He'll help you. Ask Him.] *In all your ways acknowledge Him, and He shall direct your paths."*

Philippians 1:27 summarizes the way we should respond by saying, *"Whatever happens, conduct yourselves in a manner worthy of the gospel of Christ"* (NIV). It's not so much your circumstances that count; it's your character that makes you great. Whatever happens, make sure your everyday life is worthy of the Gospel. One of the secrets of Joseph's success is that he honored God in his everyday life; he honored God in the trivial, the mundane, the day-to-day chores.

> **It's not so much what happens to you as what happens through you.**

Does the quality of your work, right now, make an impact for the Lord? When people look at your work, do they say, "That person is top-notch! Something is different about him! It must be the Spirit of God in his life!"? Do you work for the glory of God in everything that you do? That's what Joseph did.

Some of you are right on the edge of greatness. What God could do in you and through you would be phenomenal and incredible to all of us. But you've got to start with the basics. Be responsible. Have integrity. Trust God.

## Prayer:

> Dear Lord, You are the Master Controller of circumstances. When it is easy to do less than my best, help me

to remember that I am serving You. Keep me pure, even when those around me are not. Help me to know, as Joseph knew, that You have Your hand on me. Raise me up to serve You in greater ways than I can even imagine. Thank You for being a God who lifts people from the pit to the palace. In Jesus' name, I pray. Amen.

# 6

# PROCEED WITH PASSION

T he impetus behind all great art, all great music, all great literature, all great drama, and all great architecture is passion. Passion makes things great. Passion mobilizes armies to sacrifice themselves in battle. It enables and drives scientists to find new cures for dreaded diseases. It equips athletes to break records and get to the Olympics. Passion will maximize your edge as you pursue your goals in life. Nothing great is done without passion.

Passion turns the unbelievable into the doable. It energizes life. It gives zest, zeal, vitality, and drive. It makes you feel truly and radiantly alive. Without passion, days are dull, hours are drab, and moments are filled with boredom. God wants you and me to live passionate lives.

God wants us to sense the passion that He has placed within us by His grace. As we embrace this new century, as we navigate the challenges that lie ahead, God wants us to live not pathetically, not pitifully, but passionately. One day a scribe walked up to Jesus. He was impressed by what he had heard Jesus say, and he had an important question to ask Him. Here's my version of their conversation:

> The scribe said, "Jesus, what's the most important commandment? What's the one thing I need to grasp if I don't get any of the others down?"

Jesus said, "I'm going to summarize the Scriptures. I'm going to give you the *Cliffs Notes*, if you will. I'm going to supply you with the abbreviated version, and I'm going to give it to you in two sentences. If you understand these two things, you have it made. If you get these down in your life, you're going to be all right. Here it is: *"'Love the LORD your God with all your heart, with all your soul, with all your mind, and with all your strength." This is the first commandment. And the second, like it, is this: "You shall love your neighbor as yourself." There is no other commandment greater than these'* (Mark 12:30–31)."

Can you hear and feel the passion in those verses? Jesus says there are really only two things that matter in life: loving God and loving people. Those are the things that matter most. Loving God and loving people.

I think one way to paraphrase verse 30 would be, "Love the Lord with all your passion, all your prayer, all your intelligence, and all your energy." In other words, don't love people and God in a halfhearted way. Do it passionately. Give it all you've got. Loving in this way is not for wimps.

**Passion turns the impossible into the possible.**

If you want to fulfill your destiny, if you want to live a successful life, you have to live with passion, because life deserves and demands everything you've got. If you desire to maximize your impact; if you want to meet the unanticipated possibilities, unlimited opportunities, and unexpected challenges that life brings, you are going to have to live passionately.

There are things worth being passionate over. The Bible uses this phrase *"with all your heart"* over and over again. The Scriptures say we're to seek God passionately, with all our hearts. The Bible tells us we're to love God passionately. It says that we're to serve God passionately, follow Him passionately, and trust Him passionately.

# Proceed with Passion

In Colossians 3:23 Paul said, *"Whatever you do, do it heartily, as to the Lord and not to men."* This verse teaches us that no matter what we do, we should do it passionately. Never do anything half-heartedly. If you're going to do something, it's worth doing it with all your heart. If you're going to do it halfheartedly, why bother doing it at all?

In America, we are often passionate about everything *but* God. We are passionate about sports. We are passionate about the movies we watch. We are passionate about the clothes we wear. We are passionate about certain kinds of cars. We are passionate about restaurants—some of us more than others. Some time ago, I was on the Internet, and I tapped into Amazon.com, that giant online bookstore. I was trying to find every book that had the word *passion* in its title.

I discovered that literally thousands of books have the word *passion* somewhere in their titles. I narrowed the search to the words *a passion for.* Here are some of the books you can order: *A Passion for Birds, A Passion for Books, A Passion for Cactus, A Passion for Chocolate, A Passion for Fashion, A Passion for Fish.* The list goes on to include: *Flying, Gardening, Golf, Hunting, Jazz,* even *A Passion for Mushrooms, Needlepoint, Pasta, Ponies, Potatoes, Roses, Shoes,* and, would you believe, *A Passion for Steam?*

The amazing thing in our culture is that it's perfectly appropriate to be passionate about anything and everything—except God. I can go to any sporting event and yell, scream my head off, jump up and down, and raise my hands in the air. When my team loses, I can cry; and when we win, I can dance around, and people will say, "It's all right. He's just a fan!"

However, if I go to church and do *any* of that—if I shout, holler, or jump up and run around the auditorium because God has been good to me—people say, "There's a fanatic!" They act as if it's not appropriate to get excited, be enthusiastic, or have a passion for God. Yet Jesus said in various ways, "If you're going to follow Me, you have to do it with passion." We must follow God with all our hearts. Would you describe yourself as a passionate worshipper?

Romans 12:11 teaches, *"Never be lacking in zeal, but keep your spiritual fervor"* (NIV). Circle *"keep."* That means it's not automatic. You don't stay on fire for God automatically. Passion must be maintained. You must cultivate the fire and fan the flame in order to maintain your spiritual passion.

Passion has nothing to do with age. I know plenty of passionate older folks. I know little kids who are passionate. Passion has nothing to do with personality; you do not have to be an extrovert to be passionate. I know some very passionate introverts. There's an intensity about them. There's a focal point for their energies.

You and I were born with an innate, God-given sense of passion. We were wired that way. God gave us feelings. He gave us emotions. He created us to be able to feel all that happens in the world. Our emotional makeup is what makes us different from animals. We were naturally born with passion, but years of socialization have caused us to suppress our feelings. We keep a lid on our emotions in public, but passion is natural to human beings.

Just look at little kids. They couldn't hide a feeling if they had to. They're extremely passionate. They feel everything very deeply—from the highs to the lows. There's nothing in between. It doesn't matter where kids are or what's going on. If they're upset, you're going to know it; and if they're happy, you're going to know it. What happened to us adults? Where did our zest go? What happened to our zip and our enthusiasm for life?

Some of you can remember the day you graduated from high school. That was a pretty passionate day for many of us because we didn't come out *cum laude*—we came out, "Thank You, Lawdy!" All of the required education was now behind you. Any more you received would be completely on your own; you would choose to do it. As a high school graduate, you thought, "The world is my apple, and I'm going to pick it. The world is my cake, and I'm going to eat it. It's mine for the taking. Watch out, world! Here I come!" You had great hope, great enthusiasm, and great passion as you entered adult life. What happened?

After a while, that initial passion, zest, zip, and joy began to fade. Life became so daily, so mundane, and so boring with the same routine day in, day out. Over time, our dreams gathered dust, and we lost our enthusiasm.

It's a predictable pattern. The first thing that happens is that we get the blahs. The second thing that happens is we begin to lower our expectations in life. The third thing that transpires is that we begin to question what is happening around us. Inevitably, we begin to develop aches and pains. Finally, we get a full-blown case of depression.

What happened? Why don't you have the enthusiasm you used to have? Why don't you still feel the same way about your career as you used to? Why don't you feel the same enthusiasm about your marriage that you used to? Why aren't you as close to God and on fire for God as you used to be? You have fallen prey to a passion killer.

**Beware of life's passion killers.**

I believe there are at least seven passion killers in life—people, pressures, and predicaments that will drain you dry, just sap all the life and vitality right out of you. They are passion killers. As you read the rest of this chapter, ask yourself, "Why do I have the blues? Why have I lost my zest? Why am I not passionate like I used to be? Where did my enthusiasm and excitement for God go?" Chances are, a passion killer has caught you. Are you ready for this?

## Passion Killer #1: An Unclear Purpose

Living without purpose is *the* most common reason people lack passion. Without a purpose for living, why bother? Why put forth the effort? Why get out of bed in the morning? If you have no reason for using energy, why expend it? Life seems pretty futile, if you don't know your purpose. The longer you go without clarifying God's purpose for your life, the less passion you're going to have.

Without purpose, life is passionless. Without passion, purpose is

**Passion and purpose go together.**

pointless. Passionate purpose gives you enthusiasm over the long haul. Without it, life seems futile. Isaiah said on one occasion, *"I have labored to no purpose; I have spent my strength in vain and for nothing"* (Isa. 49:4 NIV). Have you ever felt like that? Without purpose, you have no passion.

On the other hand, a clear purpose creates passion. The greater your purpose in life, the more passionate you're going to be about living, the more fully alive you're going to be. If you have an insignificant purpose—"I live for myself"—then you're not going to have much passion in life. If you have a medium-sized purpose, then you'll have a medium, moderate amount of passion.

God's purpose for your life entails everything God created you to be. You are a unique part of the ever-expanding kingdom of God. You are a conduit for the current of eternity. However, in order to access this supernatural power, you have to be connected. You must commit yourself to God's eternal, unfolding, ongoing purpose for your life and share the good news of grace, goodness, purpose, and peace with other people. As you live in the purpose of God, you will be embraced by an incredible sense of passion in your life.

There's nothing more significant than being what God made you to be, doing what God made you to do, thinking as God made you to think, and sharing in the greatest cause in the world: the advancement of the kingdom of God. There is no greater cause, and being a part of it creates the greatest amount of passion in life.

Passion is waking in the morning and bounding out of bed because you're anxious to get back to what you love to do. You're called to do it. It's something you believe in, something bigger than you alone. You're good at it, and you can hardly wait to get started at it again. It's something you'd rather be doing more than anything else in the whole world. Hopefully, it's something that makes the world a better place for other people—not just yourself. An unclear purpose will kill the passion in your life.

## Passion Killer #2: An Unemployed Talent

God has not given anybody everything, but God has given everybody something. Did you get that? God has given you certain gifts, talents, and abilities for a specific purpose. If you are stuck in a job or a career that ignores or minimizes your talent, it's no surprise that you're not passionate about it. We all are prone to become bored when our talent is not tapped or our skills are not utilized.

I have heard that up to 70 percent of all Americans are in the wrong job. They're in jobs that they're not shaped for, jobs that do not use their potential, or utilize their talents. If you have a job that uses only 30 percent of your talent, ability, and brainpower, that leaves a 70 percent boredom factor. It's no surprise that we lack passion if we're not being used in the way God intended.

You will never find a job or career than uses 100 percent of your talent because God never meant for us to find total fulfillment just in a career. That's why you need to have a ministry where you're doing something outside of your career, using talents that you're not using at work in ways that will build the body of Christ and bless the world. It should be a ministry you do out of the sheer joy of using your talents.

God put us on the planet for a purpose. God has places for us to occupy, roles for us to play, and niches for us to fill. You can discover your niche by learning what you're good at, by identifying your talents. When you find out what you're good at, that's the first step to discovering what God wants you to do in this world. First Corinthians 7:17 instructs, *"But as God has distributed to each one, as the Lord has called each one, so let him walk."* Discover what you're good at; then find the place where you can use your gifts.

If you are in a job that is draining the passion out of your life because it's not using your gifts and potential, get out! Your life is far more important than that job. You live in America, where you have a choice. You don't make these changes overnight. You have to plan for them. Prepare for them by thinking,

> A year from now, I'm going to be out of here. Right now this job is putting food on the table and keeping the lights on, but I'm more than they think I am. I can't stay in this rut, because a rut is just a grave with the ends kicked out. I'm coming up out of here.

Make your plans, and then get yourself in the position where your gifts and talents can be used to the glory of almighty God. If you don't, your passion will be depleted year after year. You'll lose your joy, and you'll lose your zest.

**You don't have to be a minister to be engaged in ministry.**

One of the purposes of the church is to help you find your niche in life. God created the church to help you discover your talents and gifts. You have a mission in the world; as you pursue it, you will passionately give glory to God by doing what God created you to do.

## Passion Killer #3: An Unbalanced Schedule

Don't look any further than your Day-Timer, your Franklin Planner, or your calendar. We all struggle with overscheduling. Whether you're overworked or underworked, either way, you tend to lose your passion. Why? We need balance in our lives. We need a balance between input and output. Some people are always giving out. There's always someone who needs help. There's always someone you can serve. There's always someone with whom you can share.

Some people are always giving out, but they're never taking in, never taking the time to recharge. If you're like that, you're thinking right now, "I don't want to read this. I'm closing this book and taking a nap!" You have "compassion fatigue." If you're always giving out, it is likely that you will cease to care at all. You will stop caring about yourself, others, and eventually about God.

There's a flip side to this script. Others are always taking in—attending another seminar, going to another class, listening to another tape, studying or learning something else—but never doing anything with what they have learned. If you study the Bible and never do anything about it, eventually it creates a lack of compassion in your life. Paul said, *"The letter* [of the law] *kills, but the Spirit gives life"* (2 Cor. 3:6). The Scriptures are not just something to be studied; they are something to be done.

Fortunately, God has given us a solution to both of these problems. First Timothy 4:7–8 says it this way: *"Exercise yourself toward godliness. For bodily exercise profits a little, but godliness is profitable for all things, having promise of the life that now is and of that which is to come."* Keep yourself fit. It takes some time and some trouble to keep yourself spiritually fit. It's a great thing to be physically fit, but these verses remind us that it's even more important to be spiritually fit. Just as it takes balance to be physically fit—exercise and a balanced diet comprised of fat, carbohydrates, protein—it also takes balance in our lives to keep us spiritually fit.

You're spiritually fit as you balance these five purposes of God in your life:

> *Worship*—thinking about God, honoring Him, and praising Him for who He is
> *Fellowship*—loving other people and making a difference in their lives
> *Bible Study*—knowing God's Word and letting the message of the Bible impact our lives
> *Ministry*—touching others with love and reaching out in practical ways to meet their needs
> *Outreach*—telling other people the Good News of who God is and what He wants to do in our lives

Spiritual health comes as we balance these five purposes in our everyday lives. Lack of balance is a passion killer.

## Passion Killer #4: An Unconfessed Sin

Few things will steal our joy more quickly or rob us of our passion faster than unconfessed sin and the guilt that comes from it. What many of us do is to rationalize our sins. We don't think about our sins consciously; instead, we push them down inside us, and they affect our lives subconsciously.

In Psalm 38, David said, *"My guilt has overwhelmed me like a burden too heavy to bear....I am bowed down and brought very low; all day long I go about mourning"* (vv. 4, 6 NIV). You can't feel enthusiasm and guilt at the same time. It doesn't work.

It's like having a computer with limited random access memory. Random access memory (RAM) is what permits your computer to operate programs. If your RAM is limited and you try to run too many programs at once, the computer is going to crash. What's my point? Some of us are in the middle of a *personal system crash.* We're trying to be enthusiastic about life, but guilt is crashing our joy. We're trying to run too many programs on the terminal of our souls. Guilt and enthusiasm don't run well together. Sin and celebration don't operate well together.

How can we solve the problem of guilt? First John 1:9 says, *"If we confess our sins, He is faithful and just to forgive us our sins and to cleanse us from all unrighteousness."* All we have to do is take our sins and guilt to God, tell Him what we have done, and ask Him for forgiveness. Then we can trust God not only to forgive us, but also to cleanse us, to strengthen us, and to give us the victory. God will do exactly that.

Too many of us want to deal with our sins in installments. We know we owe. We know there's a debit on our accounts, but rather than take it *all* to God and accept the payment that Christ provides, we want to do it in installments. We want to take the minimum monthly amount to Him and keep the rest on our accounts.

I encourage you today, as soon as you know there's something wrong, take it to God immediately. Confess it, release it, and get back to living the abundant life again. The songwriter was right when he said,

> O what peace we often forfeit,
> O what needless pain we bear,
> All because we do not carry
> Ev'rything to God in prayer.[1]

Unconfessed sin is a passion killer.

## Passion Killer #5: Unresolved Conflict

Have you ever started the day by thinking, "This is going to be a great day," but then you got into a silly argument with someone over something simple, and all the zip went out of your "doo-dah"? Unresolved conflict eats away at us and drains the passion right out of us. It's like letting the air out of a tire. Life just goes flat.

Some of us are in situations at home or work where there is constant conflict. And we can't do anything about it; we can't change it. What do you do? How do you keep unresolved conflict from draining you dry?

Watch out for resentment, envy, and prolonged anger. Job 5:2 says, *"Resentment kills a fool, and envy slays the simple"* (NIV). Pay attention to the words *"resentment"* and *"envy."* Psalm 37:8 says, *"Cease from anger, and forsake wrath; do not fret; it only causes harm."* Those three parasites—resentment, envy, and anger—will drain your passion every time.

That's why the Scriptures teach us about the importance of forgiveness. God knows what resentment, envy, and anger can do to us. If we hold on to anger, if we permit ourselves to bathe in jealousy, if we immerse ourselves in resentment, we're allowing other people to control our emotions. So if I want my passion back, I have to learn to forgive. I have to be content with what I have and not be jealous over other people's positions and possessions. I have to learn to let go of anger.

## Passion Killer #6: An Unsupported Lifestyle

We were not meant to live life alone. God said right from the start, *"It is not good that man should be alone"* (Gen. 2:18). We all need each other. I'm not talking about just romantic relationships; we need authentic, meaningful, and godly friendships. God never meant for us to go through life as a solo act. Whether we are married or single, we need relationships. Human beings were made for relationships. We need each other. God wired us that way. That's why the most serious form of punishment is called solitary confinement.

We weren't made to be without other people. Whether you marry or remain single, you need support. You need people in your life who will be there when you grapple with problems. With the help of others, you can tackle certain problems that you would never be able to solve on your own.

Friends can encourage you, support you, and kick you in the seat when you need it. They can get you going. If you try to go through life on your own, without anyone's help or support, your passion is going to fade quicker than a colored cotton shirt in a bucket of bleach.

The Bible says, *"Two are better than one, because they have a good reward for their labor. For if they fall, one will lift up his companion. But woe to him who is alone when he falls, for he has no one to help him up"* (Eccl. 4:9–10). If you are not part of a small group where you are accountable to others, you're cheating yourself. Who's going to be there with you when you need help? If you think you won't ever need anybody's help, then you really do need help! You need to make some good, godly friends.

You need some brothers and sisters who will stand by you. If you try to face life alone, without anybody else helping you out, your passion is going to fade quickly. You need support.

## Passion Killer #7: An Undernourished Spirit

This passion killer is the greatest of all because it's at the root of all the others. Passion is a spiritual issue. It's a matter of the heart. You can't restore your passion with money. You can't restore it with a pill. Passion comes from within the heart. You're more than just a body. God gave you a spirit. God gave you the ability to talk with Him and commune with Him and to be passionate. You need to nourish your spirit.

Every week circumstances and situations come into our lives that conspire to shrink our hearts and shrivel our spirits. People are rude. They criticize or misjudge us. They disappoint us. Because we are alive, we're going to face, on a weekly basis, problems and pains. There are going to be some situations that worry us, and other situations that leave us utterly fatigued.

If we don't nourish our spirits, our hearts will grow cold and calloused. Our spirits will shrink and shrivel up, and in old age, we're going to be crotchety, cranky, grumpy, irascible people whom nobody likes. And we don't want that. We want to be fully alive until we hit the grave. Many people die internally before they die physically. They let their hearts and their spirits shrivel up.

What's the antidote? Intentionally nourish and feed your spirit. How do you do that? Colossians 2 says,

> *Just as you trusted Christ to save you, trust him, too, for each day's problems; live in vital union with him. Let your roots grow down into him and draw up nourishment from him. See that you go on growing in the Lord, and become strong and vigorous in the truth you were taught. Let your lives overflow with joy and thanksgiving for all he has done.*
>
> (Col. 2:6–7 TLB)

If you want to proceed with passion, get plugged in to God. Develop a daily, vital, growing, vibrant relationship with Jesus Christ. Spend time with God in prayer and in studying His Word so that your spiritual roots grow deep. Then you will continue to be restored and renewed spiritually on a day-to-day basis. You have to receive a fresh infilling from Him so that you have something to give to others.

God is a passionate God, and He wants us to live passionately. Did you know that God is passionate about getting to know you? Exodus 34:14 says, *"You must worship no other gods, but only the LORD, for he is a God who is passionate about his relationship with you"* (NLT).

I know this is mind-boggling and hard to understand, but the Creator of the universe, the One who made all of nature, who made everyone in this world, wants to have a relationship with you. And it's not just something that's at the back of God's agenda—not something God does in His spare time. God is passionate about having a relationship with you.

When God says that He *"is passionate about his relationship with you,"* if you don't get excited about that, if that doesn't turn you on and wind your crank, you just don't understand. The Creator of the entire universe invites you and me into a relationship that's intimate, vital, and passionate.

What is the worst sin a Christian can commit? Adultery? Gossip? Lying? Backstabbing? Fornication? Getting high? Nope. Know what it is? The worst sin a Christian can commit is *lukewarmness*. In Revelation 3:15, Jesus says to those who are already believers, *"I...wish you were cold or hot."*

Christ would rather have us be cold than lukewarm. Why? Jesus says, *"Because you are lukewarm, and neither cold not hot, I will vomit you out of My mouth"* (v. 16). This text is literally rendered, "It makes me want to throw up!" That's how serious God is. Polite translations say, *"I will spue thee out of my mouth"* (KJV); *"I am about to spit you out of my mouth"* (NIV). The worst sin for a believer is being lukewarm. Christ says, *"I...wish you were cold or hot"* (v. 15).

## Proceed with Passion

If Jesus is whom He says He is, if He saved you, if He did what He said He was going to do, if God's Word is true, it deserves everything you have.

Jesus is not a piece of the pie along with your career and hobbies. He is the whole pie. If that is not true, then let's close up shop, sit on the couch, and watch golf on TV! Christianity *cannot be* moderately important. A casual Christian is a contradiction in terms. You're either passionate about God or you're not.

Why aren't you more passionate about God? Is it because you don't really know Him or somewhere along the way you lost touch with Him? The more you know God, the more you love Him. The more you understand what God has done for you, the more passionate you're going to be about loving Him with all your heart, soul, mind, and strength. Get to know God.

The people who make the greatest impact are passionate people—not the smartest, the wealthiest, the most beautiful, or the best educated, but the most passionate. Passionate people are world changers. If you're going to maximize your edge and navigate the challenges of life, you're going to have to be passionate.

Where does passion come from? Gratitude. Do you have anything to be grateful for? I think so. As you come to Christ in faith, God is willing to forgive every sin, every mistake you've ever committed. Aren't you glad that God has made you for a purpose? Aren't you glad that there is meaning and significance to life? Aren't you glad that you're not here by accident; you're here on purpose!

God promises that, as you trust Him, love Him, and walk with Him He will give you abundant life while you're here and eternal life when you die. He offers an eternal assurance that you will make it to heaven. It's guaranteed by grace.

If the fireworks in your spirit are all wet, I can tell you how to dry them out, how to get the passion flowing in your spirit, how to recapture your enthusiasm and be fully alive: go back to gratitude.

Remember what God has done for you. Start nourishing your spirit again. Start spending time in the five things that will bring balance and health to your heart: You need to *worship* every week. You need to *study your Bible* every week. You need to *fellowship with other believers* in a small group. You need *a ministry* where you're using your gifts to help other people. You need *a life mission* in the world that testifies to those who are around you.

Don't just *take* time, but *make* time to nourish your spirit, because no one else is going to do it for you. If you don't nourish your spirit, it will shrivel, your heart will shrink, and you will grow cold. The twenty-first century is here! Proceed with passion.

Some of you are in crisis mode today. What passion killer is robbing you of your joy? Why don't you pray this prayer?

## Prayer:

> Gracious God, I want passion and enthusiasm in my life again. I want to get up in the morning and look forward to the day ahead. I want to love You passionately, and I want to love others passionately. I want to be fully alive until I die. Restore the joy of my salvation. Help me to remember all that You have done for me.
>
> Thank You for forgiving my sins. Thank You for creating me on purpose. Jesus, be the Lord of my life. Help me to take the time and trouble to nourish my spirit every day, spending time getting to know You better. Give me the power to make the course corrections that I need in order to live a more passionate life. In Your name, I pray. Amen.

# 7

# LIVE IN LOVE

Have you noticed how confused our world is about love? We want love, and we need love; however, we are confused about and afraid of love. Men want "fire in their bellies," but none in their hearts. Two books make this clear: *Fire in the Belly: On Being a Man* by Sam Keen[1] and *Iron John: A Book about Men* by Robert Bly.[2] Both books treat the chronic difficulty that men have in feeling and expressing love. The authors write that men in particular are afraid to show love, fearing that it will be interpreted as weakness or that their sexual orientation will be questioned.

Women, too, are afraid to express love, fearing that, if they do, they will be rendered vulnerable, susceptible, defenseless, and misunderstood. Nations are afraid that if they speak of love, they will become assailable to their enemies. Politicians believe that if they speak of love, somebody will think they are wimps. Even church folks feel that if they make love supreme, they will be seen as lacking in discipline, decisiveness, and direction. Love is not receiving the emphasis that it should in our lives.

How many Christians are or have been known primarily as people of love? How many churches have made love the chief criterion for church membership or the first requirement for leadership in the church? What is it that people think about when they attempt to define the essence of their faith or the character of the people of God? What is the first thing we think about when we must explain to others who we are and why we do what we do?

I must honestly confess that often when I am called to describe the quality of the church or the character of the denomination of which I am a part, I do not give love first place in my descriptions, definitions, and explanations. It just doesn't come to mind. I wonder how many churches in their orientation of new members explain and expound upon the need for love to be explicit, expressed, and emphatic. When I read about the history and tenets of people of faith across the globe, often love does not appear at all.

Many denominations do not include love as a primary focus in their articles of faith. Their lists may include things like baptism by immersion, separation between church and state, local autonomy, the Bible as the only rule of faith and practice, freedom of conscience, the priesthood of all believers—but nothing about love. To be sure, love stands like a shadow behind each of these principles, breathing into them the breath of life and making them last through the storms and changes of many centuries. Love is always around, though it is seldom seen, celebrated, or even mentioned.

We hesitate to talk about love. I wonder if it is our reverence for love that prompts us to avoid speaking about the ways in which we should love each other, or is it not our failure to live in love that causes us to keep silent on the subject?

Perhaps we fail to live in love because it seems too simple, too sentimental, too lenient. We are prone to prefer the disciplines of truth and the enforcements of power to the actions of love and the persuasions of grace. Even among people of faith, we find it more convenient to be identified by the Book we carry than by the love we are to show. The great New Testament scholar C. H. Dodd declares that there is no real New Testament experience that does not express itself in love.[3] And yet, to our shame, love is perhaps the most neglected power, discipline, and phenomenon in the church today.

It is not mentioned in our creeds, rehearsed in our rituals, demonstrated in our devotions, central in our prayers, or practiced in our procedures. We would rather follow the dictates of *Robert's*

*Rules of Order* than obey Jesus' command, *"Love one another"* (John 13:34). We would rather boast about our numbers than build up our love. We would rather make our budget larger than make our love greater. We would rather quote the Bible and show off our spiritual gifts than live our love and display graceful hospitality.

American preacher Charles Jefferson once said, "The great tragedy of the ages is that after two thousand years of grace, Christianity has not yet been identified with love." Few, if any, congregations have been trained in any denomination anywhere to repeat Sunday after Sunday, "I believe in the new commandment to love God with all my heart, soul, and strength, and to love my neighbor as myself."

We have trained people to tithe, to speak in tongues, to dance, to shout, to teach, to witness, to discern, to vote, to serve, to preside, to sing, and to direct, but we have not taught them how to love. We have been taught how to *act* like Christians, but not how to *be* Christians. If the church through twenty centuries had kept the commandment to love at the forefront of its preaching and practice, what a difference it would have made in the world.

Slavery would have been abolished in the first century. Oppression would have been wiped from the face of the planet. Discrimination because of race, class, and gender would have been unknown. Governments would have been consecrated. Economic systems would have been transformed. The poor would have been helped. The rich would have been challenged to give. Drive-bys would now be stop-bys.

Drugs would have been used constructively and not destructively. Babies would have been born into families where they were loved and protected, not abused and neglected. Domestic violence would have been eliminated. All these things would have occurred if the *church* had only kept love at the forefront of its practices and proclamations.

**What does it mean to love?**

People are confused about love because the word *love* has been batted about and abused. It can now mean anything from the most frivolous impulse to the deepest and most sublime commitment. We use the word for so many different things. I love my wife, I love America, I love hot dogs—and football, ice cream, nice cars, my dog, and even tacos. I love the flag. We love so many different things.

There is a lot of misconception about what real love is. Some people think love is a feeling. Love conveys feeling, but it is not in and of itself a feeling. Too often we think love is an ocean of emotion, a quiver in my liver, goose bumps on the back of my neck—an emotion I can't handle. No doubt about it: love causes feelings, but love is not a feeling. It's much more than that.

Another misconception is that love is uncontrollable. In other words, you can't handle it. "I fell in love" means "I had no control over it." You hear people say things like, "I can't help it; I'm in love," or, sadly, "I can't help it; I just don't love him anymore"—as if love were uncontrollable. The Scriptures teach us differently. The Scriptures declare that love is at least two things.

## Love Is a Choice

Colossians 3:14 says, *"Above all these things put on love, which is the bond of perfection."* It's something you put on like a coat. It's a choice. It's the commitment to care, and it is controllable. You choose whom you will love and whom you will not love.

## Love Is a Way of Life

Love is something you do. It's more than just feelings. It's more than just words. First John 3:18 encourages us by saying, *"Let us not love in word or in tongue, but in deed and in truth."* Notice that love is something you do. It is a behavior. It's not just talk. A man said to his fiancée, "Baby, I would die for you." She said, "You're always saying that, why don't you do it?" Love is something you do; it's an action, an effort. It's more than words or talk.

If love were just a feeling, then it could not be commanded. Have you ever tried to command a feeling? You can't command a feeling. You can't force a feeling. Love is not a feeling. It's something you do; it's a choice and an action. Therefore, it's possible to love people you don't like. Let there be no mistake: as we seek to live our lives, there will be plenty of people who don't like us and whom we don't like.

Jesus never demanded or commanded that we have to have "warm fuzzies" about everybody, but He did command us to love everybody. We are to make the choice, then practice the conduct of love. We may not like the way people act, the way they dress, the way they talk, or the way they smell, yet we can still love them through the power of Christ.

Winston Churchill and Lady Astor had a famous rivalry. One day Lady Astor said, "Winston, if I were married to you I'd put poison in your coffee." Churchill replied, "Nancy, if I were married to you, I'd drink it." On another occasion, Lady Astor told Churchill, "Why, Sir Churchill, you are drunk!" Churchill responded, "And you are ugly, but I shall be sober in the morning!"

No matter how challenging or difficult it is, the good news is that each of us can begin today to *live in love* from this moment forward. How do you do it?

## Experience God's Love Personally

There is no time at which God does not love you. Isn't that good news? You need to accept God's love and let Him love you. You need to feel and understand how deeply He loves you. Ephesians 3:17–19 says in *The Living Bible,*

> *I pray that Christ will be more and more at home in your hearts, living within you as you trust in him. May your roots go down deep into the soil of God's marvelous love; and may you be able to feel and understand, as all God's children*

*should, how long, how wide, how deep, and how high his love really is; and to experience this love for yourselves.*

Circle the words *"feel"* and *"understand."* Those words are very important. God does not want us to know just intellectually and cerebrally that He loves us. He wants us to really feel His love for us deep down in our hearts, at the roots of our beings. Why is that so important? When people act unlovingly, it's because they feel unloved.

Hurting people are the people who will hurt you. People who are unloving are feeling unloved themselves. The starting point, before you can ever love anybody else, is to begin to understand how much God loves you, how much you matter to God. Don't forget that.

## Forgive Those Who Have Hurt You

Colossians 3:13 says, *"Forgive whatever grievances you may have against one another. Forgive as the Lord forgave you"* (NIV). Why? It is impossible to love one person while hating somebody else. I cannot love my kids fully if I'm still resenting my parents. I can't love my wife fully if I'm still reacting to my former girlfriend. I cannot love somebody and be resentful toward somebody else at the same time.

A bitter heart is a divided heart. Somebody says, "Why can't I love my husband?" You're still holding on to the past. "Why can't I love my wife?" You're still reacting to the past. You have to let it go. It's not fair to those around you. You have to let go so that you can start to grow.

**Let go so you can grow.**

Statistics tell us that one out of every three women will be abused in her lifetime. One out of every seven men will be abused in his lifetime. You have to let go and forgive others. A divided heart is a resentful heart. You cannot fully love somebody else if you're still reacting to somebody or something that happened in the past.

Two brothers, Harry and James, were playing upstairs. Somehow James hit Harry with a stick, and they started to fight. Tears and accusations followed, and this behavior continued until bedtime. When their Mom came upstairs and found out what happened, she said, "Now, Harry, you're going to have to forgive James for hitting you." Harry asked, "Do I have to do it tonight?"

She said, "Yes, the Bible says, *'Do not let the sun go down on your wrath'* (Eph. 4:26)." Harry thought for a minute, then said, "Okay. I'm going to forgive him tonight, but when we wake up tomorrow, he'd better watch out." You need to forgive those who have hurt you. Yet to do this, you must experience God's love. Jesus said, *"Love one another as I have loved you"* (John 15:12).

Until you realize how much Jesus loves you, you will not know how to love others. Jesus said, *"If you forgive men when they sin against you, your heavenly Father will also forgive you. But if you do not forgive men their sins, your Father will not forgive your sins"* (Matt. 6:14–15 NIV). When you think about how much God has forgiven you, then you can forgive others.

## Think Loving Thoughts

Philippians 2:4–5 says, *"Let each of you look out not only for his own interests, but also for the interests of others. Let this mind be in you which was also in Christ Jesus."* How do you think loving thoughts toward an unloving person? Do you know that God often puts us in the company of unloving people to teach us how to really extend love? It's easy to love people who are just like you, but God teaches us real love by putting us around unlovable people.

How do we learn to think loving thoughts toward that kind of people? By focusing on their hurts, their problems, and their needs. I know it sounds crazy, but this is the way of transformation. You begin to say to yourself, "What are their hurts, their problems, and their needs?" You don't think just of your own affairs.

**Hurting people hurt people.**

You keep looking and asking, "Where are they hurting? What do they need?" It's easier to love them when you look beyond the hurtful things they do, see where they hurt, and minister to their pain.

Those who deserve your love the least are those who need it the most. They need massive doses of love in order to have their emotions healed and their relationships restored. My prayer is that the church I serve would be a place where massive doses of love are given to people who hurt. Do you want to be part of a church like that? Then let love begin with you.

Most of us are more interested in being loved than in giving love. Our thoughts determine the way we feel, and the way we feel determines the way we act. If I act unlovingly, it's because I feel unloved. We feel unloved because we are thinking unloving thoughts. We cannot force a feeling! We have to start with the way we think. As we change our thoughts, we will change our feelings.

Don't try to force your feelings. Become sympathetic to those around you who hurt, and try to see things from their perspective so that you might minister to their needs. Just as a train follows its engine, your feelings will follow your commitment. Think loving thoughts.

## Act in a Loving Way

Love is more than a feeling. There is no real, authentic, or holy love that does not express itself in positive, constructive, life-enhancing action. Love is an action. Don't just *say* you love someone; *show* your love by *what you do*. This principle applies even to people you dislike, to people who make you sick, to people you hate being around or perhaps cannot even stand. Act lovingly toward them.

Live in Love

Love is an action. It is not hypocritical to act in loving ways toward a person, even though you may not feel loving toward him or her: it's loving in advance of feeling. Remember, it's easier to act your way into a feeling than to feel your way into an action. As we take faith-based action, even though we may not feel like it, eventually our feelings will follow.

Some husbands say, "When I feel considerate toward my wife, then I'll start acting considerately!" You'll have to wait a long time for that to happen! You must seize the initiative by your actions. Some wives say, "When I feel romantic toward my husband, then I'll start acting romantically again toward him!" Unfortunately, it is not going to happen, ladies. Act your way into a feeling; do not try to feel your way into an action.

**Loving in advance is faith on display.**

You cannot change a feeling by force. You have to change your feelings by changing your thoughts. That action will amend your feelings. Begin to act in loving ways. In Luke 6:27–28, Jesus gives us a poignant command: *"Love your enemies, do good to those who hate you, bless those who curse you, and pray for those who spitefully use you."* These four positive acts are very specific and will enable us to handle people who "rack our nerves" and people with whom it is difficult to cope.

This teaching is a terrific example of what psychologists call "positive assertiveness." Assertiveness means "choosing the way I want to respond rather than simply reacting to you." All of us are either actors or reactors. If you're an actor, you initiate. If you're a reactor, you just recreate. If somebody hurts you, you hurt them back. If somebody says something bad to you, you say something bad back. Anybody can do that.

Anyone can react in the same way that others have reacted to him, but "positive assertiveness" is when you choose your response. You seize the initiative, and you say to yourself,

> I'm going to be the better person. I'm going to take the
> high road. I'm not going to let that individual push my

109

buttons. I'm not going to let him yank my chain. I'm not going to be controlled by his negativity. I'm not going to be sucked into his nastiness. I refuse to let him steal my joy, block my blessing, hinder my progress, or distract my mind. I'm going to assert myself and do the right thing no matter what he does or says to me.

This permits you to stay in control. When other people are making you angry, they are in control. When you choose your response, you're in control. Jesus teaches us four responses to handle those who would hurt us.

## Love Them

*"Love your enemies"* (Luke 6:27). How do you love your enemies? On a personal level, you overlook their faults. That's the loving thing to do. The Bible says in Ephesians 4:2, *"Be patient with each other, making allowance for each other's faults because of your love"* (TLB). People who are mature do not "rub it in"; they try to "rub it out."

## Do Good

*"Do good to those who hate you, bless those who curse you, and pray for those who spitefully use you"* (Luke 6:27–28). This means you look for ways to give, to help, to be positive, and to respond positively. You can give without loving, but you cannot love without giving. Love is giving. What do you do with that person who is an irritant, whom you're having a hard time getting along with? You go the second mile. You make the loving response. You offer practical help. You do him or her a favor.

Husband, are you having a difficult time with your wife? Go home and blow her mind: cook dinner—or take some home; wash the dishes; pick up your clothes. When she regains consciousness after fainting from the shock, all you have to do is smile and say, "I love you."

Lady, surprise your husband—even if he's difficult to talk to or connect with, even if he just doesn't seem to understand what you need or want. Make up your mind that you're going to minister to him. Purpose to do something unusually nice for him. Jesus said, *"Do good…hoping for nothing in return; and your reward will be great"* (Luke 6:35).

## Bless Those Who Curse You

Speak kindly and positively. Guard what you say, especially when you're talking to people who don't know how to talk to you. Have you ever had that type of conversation? Have you ever conversed with someone who really didn't talk to you with respect? If so, this text speaks directly to you: build up people who put you down.

When your mate is criticizing you, build him or her up. Don't get into a criticism contest; don't get into a fighting match. Be assertive. Choose the right response. Bless those who curse you. What can you say that's positive in the situation? It may take a little ingenuity, a little creativity, and a whole lot of the grace of God, but you can do it. What can you say that's positive about your mate? Encourage your spouse.

## Pray for Those Who Mistreat You

Pray for those who hurt you. This act will change both of you. If you want to change your mate or someone with whom you are in a relationship, start praying for him or her. Prayer will not only change that person, it will also change you. Over the long haul, you cannot pray for and hate someone at the same time. If you start praying for somebody at work whom you despise, your attitude will change. You cannot pray for and despise someone at the same time.

Remember the story of Job in the Old Testament? Job lost everything—his children, his wealth, his health. All he had left was a nagging wife. He had three so-called friends who were critical of him. With friends like Job's, who needs enemies! All three essentially said to him, "Job, your problem is that you're a sinner;

you're having bad things happen to you because you're a bad person." That's bad theology even in this century!

A lot of bad things happen to good people, and they are not all the result of personal sin. Job's compatriots came to criticize him. The Bible says in the last chapter of Job that God healed Job, blessed him with seven sons and three daughters, and restored all his wealth, giving him *"twice as much as he had before"* (Job 42:10). These blessings came *after* he had prayed for his critics—the very people who were criticizing him and putting him down. The Bible says, *"After Job had prayed for his friends, the LORD made him prosperous again"* (v. 10 NIV). The teaching is plain: if you care about other people, God will take care of your needs.

You must choose to act in loving ways. Right now, I want you to think about those people in your life who are giving you the most trouble: at home, on your job, in the church, in your group. Can I give you a prayer that may help?

> God, right now I need You to fill me with Your love. I know that You love me. Help me right now to forgive those who have hurt me. Help me to start thinking loving thoughts about them and doing loving deeds for them. In Jesus' name, Amen.

First Corinthians 13 is the classic chapter on love in the Bible. It's the one everybody should study to learn how to become a great lover. It says, *"Love is patient, love is kind. It does not envy, it does not boast, it is not proud. It is not rude, it is not self-seeking, it is not easily angered, it keeps no record of wrongs"* (vv. 4–5 NIV). Do you keep a record of wrongs so that you can use it against other people? That's not the loving thing to do. *"Love does not delight in evil but rejoices with the truth. It always protects, always trusts, always hopes, always perseveres. Love never fails"* (vv. 6–8 NIV).

If you were to study this chapter, you would find that there are fifteen actions—things to do—because love is something you do. It is not a feeling; it is a way of acting toward people. It's patient, it's kind, it's not rude, and so on. All fifteen of these actions are ways you can learn to be loving.

## Expect the Best from Others

First Corinthians 13:7 in *The Living Bible* says, *"If you love someone you will be loyal to him no matter what the cost. You will always believe in him, always expect the best of him, and always stand your ground in defending him."* Circle *"expect the best."* We tend to live up to what other people expect of us. Dads, if you say to your kids, "You're really dumb!" do you think that's going to make them smarter? Ladies, if you say to your husbands, "You're really lazy, aren't you?" do you think that's going to make them take the initiative and get busy? Men, if you say to your wives, "You are really boring," do you think that's going to make them more exciting?

Labeling only reinforces the negative. It never changes anybody. Nagging doesn't work. The goal is to speak positively to people. If you want to change yourself, your family, or your mate, then treat them the way you want them to become. Did you get that? Expect the best of them. Raise the level of expectation, and watch people blossom under the sunlight of affirmation and expectation. Treat them the way you want them to become. That's the secret.

> **Treat people the way you want them to become.**

Perhaps as you read this chapter, you're saying to yourself, "Lance, that's good and all, but my relationship is dead. The feelings are gone. There are no feelings left. We've said and done some painful things to each other, and there's nothing left." What do you do in that kind of situation? Do you just give up? Do you just walk away? No, you pray for a resurrection—not for resuscitation, but for a resurrection. Not for the old life you had, but for a new life unlike anything you've ever known.

## Pray for a Resurrection

How do you restore feelings that have grown cold? In Revelation 2:4–5, God is speaking to the church at Ephesus about lost love, and He instructs them to do three things. (See Revelation 2:4–5.) No matter who we are, we will all need this text someday. Human love runs out. There's a limit to how much pain any single person can take. We need more than human love to make a relationship last. Just look at the divorce record. Here are three principles to apply in our interpersonal relationships. What do you do when love has been lost?

## Remember

The first thing you do if you want to rebuild a relationship, if you want to rebuild those feelings toward a person, is to start remembering the "good old days." Focus on those happy times. Restoring relationships starts with thinking. You change the way you think. Remember all the good times you had together. Start thinking about when the relationship was rewarding and beneficial, and both of you were excited to share it. Remember the way it used to be.

You move toward what you focus on. If you focus on the junk, you're moving toward it. If you focus on the way it used to be, the thrill and the joy, you are moving toward that. Every relationship has some garbage in it. It's all a matter of where we choose to focus. Start by remembering the good times. Let those thoughts come into your mind, because those kinds of things eventually produce feelings. Those good memories, those shared events when you were close and happy, will create interest and attraction. Start there. Then move to the next step.

## Repent

The word *repent* in the Greek language is the word *metanoia*— *meta* meaning "about" and *noia* meaning "mind." When we assemble these parts, we arrive at "a change in our minds." Repentance simply means to change your mind. When I repented, I changed my mind about a lot of things. I changed my mind about God, about myself, about other people, and about the world. It was a radical redirection. It was a choice that I made in choosing radical redirection. It was a choice that I made in choosing to think in a new way.

You cannot change the way you feel toward a person. But remember that feelings are fickle and highly unreliable. You can get a feeling from a bad pizza! Only immature people live by their feelings. The mark of your maturity is when you live by your commitments, not by your feelings—when you do something because it's the right thing to do, not because it feels good.

Our culture assumes that if feelings are absent, we are exempt from responsibility. "I didn't feel it, so I didn't do it!" But as people of faith, we are to repent of that kind of attitude. We can change our feelings—not directly, but indirectly. We change our feelings toward people by changing the way we think. Stop fantasizing about what could have been, and deal with what is.

You say, "But, Lance, I just don't know how to love my wife, my husband, my siblings, my parents, my coworkers, people in the church!" I say to you: read the Manual! The answer is right there in God's Word: *"Love is kind"* (1 Cor. 13:4 NIV). Start being kind. *"Love is patient"* (v. 4 NIV). Start being patient. Love is an action, not a feeling. Remember, repent, and then go to step three.

## Restart

As the text teaches, *"Do the things you did at first"* (Rev. 2:5 NIV). You take action. Love is something you do. Work at it. As one writer has said, "The grass is not greener on the other side of the fence; the grass is greener where you water it." Did you get that?

If we would divert just half the time we spend complaining to acting in a loving way and praying, talking, and thinking in loving ways, we'd get three times the results in our relationships. Restart. Use that

**Love works if you work it.**

energy. It is easier to act your way into a feeling than to feel your way into an action.

God is in the business of resurrecting relationships. If you'll be assertive in the way the Bible teaches assertiveness and choose your response, things will change. Human love is not strong enough to weather the storms in life. It runs out. It goes dry, but God's love never gives up. God's love never fails.

## Prayer:

> Loving God, help us today to experience Your love—to really feel it, not just know about it. Help us to know that we are secure in Your love. Help us to forgive those who've hurt us. Today, we release them. Help us to think loving thoughts and to see the hurts, pain, fears, and worries of others. Lord, help us to act in loving ways. Empower us to do good, to bless and pray for those who hurt us, to act in love rather than to react in anger. Help us to remember, repent, and restart in the life of love. Help us to start here, to start now. In Jesus' name, Amen.

# 8

# PURSUE YOUR PURPOSE

T he dictionary tells us that "to drive" means "to guide, control, and direct." Driving a car means that you guide, control, and direct it down the street. When you drive a nail into wood, you drive, control, and direct it into the wood. When you drive a golf ball, you, hopefully, drive, control, and direct it down the fairway. When you drive a basketball, you drive, control, and direct it into the hoop.

Every human being is driven by something. Some people are driven by guilt. Some are driven by fear. Resentment, anger, or greed drives other people. Some are driven by the past, and they permit the past to control their futures. They say, "That's just the way I am. I've always been this way." What they are really saying is, "I'm stuck."

Some people are driven by parental expectations; even though they are forty years old or older, their primary goal is still to please Mommy and Daddy and to receive their stamp of approval. Some people are driven by their peers; their number one question is, "What do other people think?" Some are driven by their partners. They're married to domineering spouses. Two becoming one does not mean that one gets sacrificed; it means that, in an unselfish, loving relationship, two share a oneness.

## Find God's purpose and pursue it.

I want to suggest that the life that really matters is a life that is being driven *by purpose, on purpose.* There is no greater goal, no nobler aim, no more fulfilling objective than to discover God's purpose for your life. Let it be your driving force, and pursue your God-given purpose with passion.

Ephesians 2:10 says, *"For we are God's workmanship, created in Christ Jesus to do good works, which God prepared in advance for us to do"* (NIV). The good news is this: God has a purpose for your life. God does not create things without a purpose. The tragedy is that most people go their entire lives without ever learning what their purpose is, never discovering their niche, never finding the place where they fit. In fact, all of us live our lives on one of three levels.

The lowest level is what I call the *survival* level. Too many people live their lives in this mode. They just barely eke out a life. They are merely existing, not really enjoying life. They put in their time and hope for the weekend. They live in the survival mode. If I were to ask them, "What's your number one goal in life?" they would say, "Right now, my number one goal is to escape to Tahiti, lie on the beach, sip refreshments, and soak up rays." They are in the survival mode. That may be all right temporarily, but it's not the way to live life—just existing and vegetating.

The next level is a little bit higher. It's what I call the *success* level. That's where many of us are today. By the world's standards, we've made it. We have a comfortable lifestyle. We have possessions, prestige, and pleasure. Life is pretty good. Most of the world would love to trade their problems for ours. We've hit the success level.

But more and more, I hear questions from successful people like this: "Lance, if I'm really so successful, why don't I feel more fulfilled?" If you've looked at the recent best-selling books, many of them have to do with the dark side of success: *Ambitious Men:*

*Their Drives, Dreams, and Delusions; Quiet Desperation: The Truth about Successful Men; Coping with the Fast Track Blues: A Survival Guide for Your Climb to the Top;* and *The Search for Meaning.*

In addition, these are the books that have been on the top-selling list for the last couple of years: *Downshifting: Reinventing Success on a Slower Track; If I'm So Successful Why Do I Feel Like a Fake?: The Imposter Phenomenon; Success Trap: Rethink Your Ambitions to Achieve Greater Personal and Professional Fulfillment; Upward Nobility: How to Succeed in Business without Losing Your Soul;* and *Is It Success? or Is It Addiction?*

What are these books saying? They're saying that ultimately success does not satisfy. By the grace of God, we must go beyond success to the third level of living—beyond survival and beyond success to *significance.* What you really need is not success, but significance. When you feel significant, you feel that your life matters, that you count. You know that you are not just taking up space and using up resources, but there's a meaning, a point, a purpose to your life. Significance is the feeling that you count.

People who've discovered significance are those who've discovered God's plan for their lives. You are one in a million—actually, one in six billion. Nobody else will ever be like you. People who feel deeply significant have zeroed in on God's plan and purpose. They know what God put them here on earth for. They have found significance. Have you found significance—not just survival or success—but significance?

The tragedy is that even many successful people feel very insignificant, because they've never reached the third level. When you look at the people who have made the greatest impact on this world, they were not necessarily the brightest, the wealthiest, or the best educated. The people who have made the biggest difference in life, for good or bad, were those who had the deepest convictions—right or wrong; they were those who were passionate and had a strong sense of purpose.

119

It does not matter whether we're talking about Jesus, Jefferson, Mao, Buddha, Marx, Martin, Malcolm, or Stalin—*purpose gives conviction.* Karl Marx was driven by the purposes of Communism. Mother Teresa was driven by the purpose of compassion. Napoleon was driven by the purpose of conquest. Jefferson was driven by the purpose of liberty. Martin Luther King, Jr., was driven by the purpose of equality. Malcolm X was driven by the purpose of social justice. Jesus was driven by the purpose of salvation, liberation, reconciliation, and transformation. Everybody is driven by something.

To be all that we were meant to be, we must discover God's purpose for our lives. We must develop it, pursue it, and let it drive us toward our God-given destiny. Let me illustrate. In the Scriptures, there are numerous examples of people who were in pursuit of purpose. Acts 13:36 says, *"When David had served God's purpose in his own generation, he fell asleep"* (NIV).

David was in pursuit of purpose. How would you like to have these words written on your tombstone? "This person served God's purpose in his generation." I don't know a better epitaph than that. Why was David a man after God's own heart? His relationship with God was a priority in his life; he worked to do what God had made him to do. Yes, David made mistakes, wrong turns, and bad decisions, but he continued to work to be the person God had made him to be. He fulfilled the purpose of God for his life.

In the New Testament, we meet Paul. Paul was a man of tremendous purpose. He was driven by the purpose of God in his life. He had a life mission from which he would not waver. He said, *"I consider my life worth nothing to me, if only I may finish the race and complete the task the Lord Jesus has given me—the task of testifying to the gospel of God's grace"* (Acts 20:24 NIV).

There is a song that only you can sing. There is a mission that only you can fulfill. There is a way that only you can walk. There is a child whom only you can teach. There is a testimony that only you can give. You are utterly unique, and no one else can take your place or fulfill your purpose.

# Pursue Your Purpose

My goal is that, by the end of this book, you will be encouraged to unearth and discover the purpose for which God gave you life. Every life has a purpose. Purpose is important because it gives you the *why* of a thing. Purpose tells you why you're here. Purpose is tied to function. It is what the maker of a thing had in mind when he or she made that thing.

Why did God make you? What gifts do you have? What talents do you possess? What passions move your heart and stir your spirit? These are all clues to your purpose. What do you find easy to do? A bird does not struggle to sing; it was created to do that. A fish does not struggle to swim; swimming is etched in its design.

The purpose of God for our lives is usually so apparent that we are likely to overlook it. It seems too simple. It does not appear obviously valuable. It's right there in your face. It's what you were born to do. It is the contribution you were designed to make.

It is the gift that you were created to offer to the rest of the world. Education can sharpen it, but education cannot give it. It is a gift of God. It is what you were "made" to do. And I want to push you and prompt you today not to rest until you have discovered God's purpose for your life.

The person who knows the *why* of his or her living can transform any *how*. When you know the purpose of a car, it does not bother you that your car does not cook, because cars were not made to cook. They were made to transport, to get you from point A to point B.

When you know the purpose of an oven, it does not upset you that the oven will not produce ice cubes. Ovens were not made to provide ice. Ovens were created to heat food. That is the purpose of an oven; that is why we buy one and why we sacrifice to have one.

Your purpose is why God made you and kept you, and why *"you were bought at a price"* (1 Cor. 6:20). Your purpose is why God has strengthened you, blessed you, enabled you, empowered you, led you, and brought you out more than once. You have a purpose to pursue.

**Pursue your purpose.** I want to challenge you to think about your purpose. Write it down, and work it out. Get it in your heart. Pen a plan for your pilgrimage. Write a statement that says, "Hello, World. *This* is why I'm here. I was not accidentally made. God made me *on purpose—for a purpose.*"

Consider these five benefits to knowing your purpose and pursuing it.

## Benefit #1: It Will Reduce Your Frustration

When they have no sense of purpose, people tend to be less patient, more uptight, and more prone to outbursts. One of the reasons we are so frustrated in life is that we live in a world of multiple choices and incredible options. Opportunities are only going to increase in this century. There will be more choices, not fewer. And that makes decision making more difficult and more frustrating. It's no longer a matter of this or that; it's a matter of hundreds of different choices.

I can get three hundred channels on cable TV and still find nothing worth watching. I can choose from over one hundred fifty different kinds of cereals to buy. Every week, three hundred new grocery items are introduced. Every year, over two hundred new magazines are added to the market. It's easy to get frustrated when there are so many choices. When you don't know your purpose, you can't make decisions easily.

James 1:6 says, *"He who doubts is like a wave of the sea driven and tossed by the wind."* Indecision is frustrating. You just get pushed back and forth and don't know where to go because you don't know your purpose. The double-minded man is not capable of holding a steady course.

He is like Alice in Wonderland, who asked the Cat which way she should go. The Cat questioned her about her desired destination. She told him that she didn't really care where she went as long as she arrived "somewhere." The Cat told her that it didn't really matter, then, which way she went. If she walked long enough, she'd eventually get "somewhere."[1]

The double-minded person is unsteady in his course because he doesn't know what he is here for. Many of us waste year after year switching back and forth from project to project. We start the year saying, "I know what will make my life meaningful." By the end of the year we conclude, "This isn't working." Then we discard that path and try to find something new. We've just wasted a year of our lives.

Life makes sense if you know where you're going. If you have already discovered God's purpose for your life, then you know where you are, and you know where you want to be. You can draw a straight line and head right toward it. You're going to have detours, setbacks, challenges, roadblocks, and bumps in the road, but you can get there a whole lot quicker when you know where you're headed. It reduces the frustration level in your life. Every time you make a decision, ask yourself, "Will this decision help me to fulfill God's purpose for my life?" If the answer is yes, do it. If not, don't do it.

Trying to live your life without knowing what God made you for is like driving in a fog. Proverbs 29:18 says, *"Where there is no vision, the people perish"* (KJV). Many of you may have felt like Isaiah when he said, *"I have labored in vain, I have spent my strength for nothing and in vain"* (Isa. 49:4). In other words, Isaiah said, "I don't know why I'm working. I spend my time, but what difference does it make? What's my purpose?" Yet Isaiah knew the secret of maintaining a steady course. He said, *"You will keep him in perfect peace, whose mind is stayed on You, because he trusts in You"* (Isa. 26:3). Peace comes from knowing your purpose in life.

# Benefit #2: It Will Increase Your Motivation

Once you know what you are here for, you have a reason to live. You will be amazed at the amount of energy you have, after you have discovered why God created you in the first place. Suddenly you will have a reason to get out of bed in the morning.

You will have a new step, a new bounce, because you're motivated to fulfill what God made you to be. Most people rarely think beyond the weekend. They live just one day at a time, day in, day out, doing the same thing. They endure the daily grind, just hoping to survive until the weekend.

Some people feel like Job when he said, *"I despise my life; I would not live forever. Let me alone; my days have no meaning"* (Job 7:16 NIV). Job had an emotional flat tire. He was saying, "I don't have any purpose, any sense in my life; therefore, it's hopeless." When you have no purpose, you have no motivation. What is the secret to energy, enthusiasm, and hope in life? The secret is to pursue your purpose.

In Jeremiah 29:11, we read: *"'For I know the plans I have for you,' declares the LORD, 'plans to prosper you and not to harm you, plans to give you hope and a future'"* (NIV). Circle the word *"hope."* God wants to give you a future and a hope. When you get that, you get enthusiasm. One writer said, "God gives every bird its food, but He doesn't throw it in the nest." The bird needs to invest energy in pursuing its food. Likewise, you have to be enthusiastic.

The word *enthusiasm* comes from two Greek words: *en* and *theos*. *Theos* is the Greek word for God. When you get *en theos*—"in God"—you will be enthusiastic. It's automatic. When you're in God, you're enthusiastic. You have no idea of all the incredible things God wants to do with your life, in your life, and through your life, if you'll just get hooked up to His plan and purpose.

I'm not talking about just being a Christian. I'm talking about being what God made you to be. Many of you are in the wrong jobs, because you are driven by somebody else's approval or are motivated by wrong desires in pursuing your career. God doesn't want you to waste your life. You have no idea of the tremendous things God wants to do for you if you line up with why God made you as an individual.

Ephesians 3:20 says that God *"is able to do exceedingly abundantly above all that we ask or think, according to the power that works in us."* I'm a pretty big dreamer, but God says, "Lance, think of the biggest dream you believe I could pull off in your life. I want you to know that I can top that. Let Me blow your mind. I can do far beyond what you think is possible in your life if you will trust Me, live with humility and integrity, and walk before Me in the way I want you to live."

> As we pursue our purpose, our motivation will increase.

## Benefit #3: It Will Allow More Concentration

You don't have time for everything. But the good news is that God doesn't expect you to do everything. On top of that, only a few things are worth doing in the first place. Selection is the name of the game for effectiveness.

Concentrate your energy on what God wants you to do—not on what everybody else in the world wants you to do. Know your purpose in life; discover why God made you. Your purpose not only defines what you're going to do, but also defines what you are not going to do. It defines not only your priorities, but also your options. Your purpose defines what business you're in as well as what's none of your business.

When asked what was the most basic thing every business owner needed to know, one highly successful management consultant answered with these two key questions: "What is your business?" and "How's business?" Every individual needs to raise these questions in his or her own life: What business did God put me on the planet to handle, and how is that business doing?

In Philippians 3:13–14, Paul said, *"One thing I do* [that's concentration]: *forgetting what is behind and straining toward what is ahead, I press on toward the goal to win the prize for which God has called me heavenward in Christ Jesus"* (NIV). Paul said that knowing his life's purpose gave his life focus. There is incredible power when you focus your life. Light diffused has no power at all, but if I focus a magnifying glass and permit the sun to shine through it, I can set paper on fire. If I focus light more intensely, it becomes a laser that can cut through steel. Light diffused has no power. Light focused has tremendous power.

I want to encourage you to start now to focus your life on the things that really count. Nothing is as powerful as a life that is lived on purpose. Most people are far too busy; consequently, they are pulled in many different directions.

Choices would be easy to make if the options were between good choices or bad ones. Our lives are filled with good things, but we can burn out from too many good things. Choosing between good and bad is a struggle for those who have not yet matured. Mature people struggle to choose between good, better, and best. What does God want to do in your life?

Many people are extremely efficient, yet you can be efficient without being effective. Efficiency is doing things right. Effectiveness is doing the right thing. God wants us to be effective, not just efficient. We can have everything in its place and a place for everything, but we may just be rearranging deck chairs on the Titanic. A balanced life requires effectiveness and not just efficiency.

Ephesians 5:15–17 says, *"See then that you walk circumspectly, not as fools but as wise, redeeming the time, because the days are evil. Therefore do not be unwise, but understand what the will of the Lord is."* Don't waste your life. Know what's important, and pay close attention. Make good use of every opportunity. Do what the Lord wants you to do. Henry David Thoreau said, "The mass of men lead lives of quiet desperation."[2] Today, most people live lives of aimless distraction, playing *Trivial Pursuit* with their lives.

Knowing your purpose in life allows you to take advantage of opportunities that are right for you. It also allows you to turn down opportunities that are not right for you. One of the greatest time management tools is learning to say, "No." You can say it when you know what God's purpose is for your life.

There are people who, because of my position, try to get me to be a crusader for all kinds of causes. It took me years to learn how to say no to appeals that were good, but for which I had no giftedness. My goal is to be single-minded, to do something well, rather than to just barely accomplish many things.

## Benefit #4: It Will Attract Cooperation

An amazing thing happens when you determine a definite direction for your life: others want to move in that direction with you. Few people really know what to do with their lives; hence, when they see someone moving definitively, they say, "That's the right direction; I want to go along, too."

Sixteen years ago when I was first invited to come and share as the pastor of the Saint Paul's Baptist Church, one of the sisters on the pulpit committee asked, "How do we know that if we call you, you won't leave in five years?" I smiled and said, "You don't. We walk by faith."

I cannot tell you how many times as a pastor that I've asked that same question of God: "Lord, how do I know that the people will support me? Where are we going to find land? Where are we going to get the money? How do I know that, if I step out here and tell them we're going to build, it will happen?" God's response to my queries was, "You don't. You walk by faith." What has sustained me is faith in God, and the hope, the belief, that great people are ready to help me, at the right time, in the right way, people I don't even know yet. My prayer is, "I promise, Lord, that I'll never give up because I don't have the help, but I will trust You, Lord, to provide."

God has resources to help us that we haven't even considered. They're multiplied by thousands of persons with all sorts of talents, concerns, and skills—contacts that God can bring into your life in order to fulfill His plan. Open your eyes and see the faces of people around you. Open your ears to hear what they're saying. Today, tomorrow, next week you will meet someone who is just the right person you need to fill the right place at just the right time. You will marvel in knowing that God has arranged it beautifully.

If your goals are good, you'll be respected. The greatest way you can help other people is to be what God made you to be. Do what God made you to do. You don't help anybody by trying to be somebody you're not, by playing a role, fulfilling an expectation, or living for the approval of others. By being whom God made you to be, serving His purpose in your generation, you honor God. He will bless you. Ezra 10:4 says, *"Rise up; this matter is in your hands. We will support you, so take courage and do it"* (NIV). As you fulfill God's purpose in your life, you will attract the cooperation of others.

If you as a leader are not living up to your potential, the people you work with are being cheated. If you as a father or mother are not living up to your potential, your children are being cheated. Leaders set roles and goals. If you don't live up to your potential, those who work with you can't either.

## Benefit #5: It Will Prepare You for God's Evaluation

God made us on purpose for a purpose. There's a purpose for our being here. God has invested certain gifts, talents, and abilities in us. He has given them to us. God doesn't expect us to use them just to make money. God expects a return on His investments. He doesn't want you and me to use these talents for selfish reasons.

One day, God is going to do an audit of our lives. The Bible says, *"We shall all stand before the judgment seat of Christ….So then each of us shall give account of himself to God"* (Rom. 14:10, 12). God wants us to pass this final test, so He has given us the answers to the questions in advance. One day when we stand before God, He is going to ask, "What did you do with My Son Jesus Christ?" and "What did you do with your life?" When I am evaluated, I want a favorable review.

God has a purpose for my life. God does not create things without a purpose. Proverbs 16:4 says, *"The Lord has made everything for his own purposes"* (TLB). That includes everything! Even pencils? Yes, pencils are made to be pencils—not screwdrivers or Q-Tips, but just to be pencils.

Pencils bring glory to God by being what they were meant to be. Roses are made to be roses. God takes pleasure in watching a rose be a rose. Dolphins are made to be dolphins. You are made to be you. God takes pleasure in watching you be you. You bring glory to God, not when you fulfill somebody else's expectation, but as you become what God meant for you to be all along.

Ephesians 1:4–5 says,

> *He chose us in Him before the foundation of the world, that we should be holy and without blame before Him in love, having predestined us to adoption as sons by Jesus Christ to Himself, according to the good pleasure of His will.*

Do you want to know how much your life matters? Ask Jesus. Jesus died with His arms outstretched on the cross, saying, "I love you this much! You matter this much." You're here for a purpose. Jesus was the greatest example of what it means to pursue one's purpose. When He came to the end of His life, He could look up to heaven and say, *"'It is finished'* (John 19:30). I've done what You told Me to do."

## Prayer:

Lord, sometimes I am driven by wrong purposes. Please forgive me for trying to take the control of my life away from You. You are my Creator. You know the purpose for which I was designed. I surrender myself to You and ask that You would mold me and use me in the way that You desire. May I move beyond the survival mode, be set free from the success mode, and find significance. Jesus, what do You want to do in and through me? I want to cooperate fully with Your plan. Thank you for being in relationship with me and for having a purpose for my life that has eternal significance.

# 9

# BUILD A BALANCED LIFE

The world functions on the principle of balance. For example, the Earth is perfectly balanced. It is tilted at 23.5 degrees and rotates around the sun at 66,700 miles per hour without any vibration. It is approximately 93 million miles away from the Sun, and scientists tell us that if it were 92 million miles away, we would burn up; if it were 94 million miles away, we would freeze to death. The Earth is in balance.

There is a delicate balance in nature. Ecologists who study the ecosystems of nature testify that we are all participants in the "circle of life." Although we sit atop the food chain, we must concern ourselves with the checks and balances of nature so that we can continue to take care of our planet and take care of one another.

In architecture, there's balance. A structure must be supported in the right way. Engineers know that if a building or a bridge isn't constructed properly and the stress of the structure isn't balanced, it will collapse.

Doctors say that when we get sick it's often because there's an imbalance in our bodies. Something is out of whack. Hemoglobin, hormones, enzymes, red and white corpuscles, electrolytes—everything has to be balanced. Health is often restored when our bodies are once again in balance.

131

In the rhythm of our lives, there must be balance. Work and play. Run and rest. Eat and fast. Get and give. Speak and listen. Watch and pray. Rejoice and reflect. In our families, in our relationships, in our communities—woven throughout the fabric of our lives—in everything we do, there is the principle of balance. As my grandmother used to say, "Too much of anything is not good for you."

## God Wants Our Personal Lives to Be Balanced

Proverbs 28:2 says, *"A man of understanding and knowledge maintains order"* (NIV). He has balance in his life. First Corinthians 14:33 adds, *"For God is not the author of confusion but of peace."* God wants things to be in balance and equilibrium.

Ecclesiastes 3:1 tells us, *"To everything there is a season, a time for every purpose under heaven."* Sometimes it's not that we are not the right person or that the situation isn't right. Sometimes things work or don't work simply because of timing. That's why we shouldn't give up on God when things go wrong. Never walk away from your dream when you suffer a setback. What God has for you is for you. What God wants to accomplish in you, no one can stop.

It's just a matter of time. You may be waiting now. You may be in a holding pattern. You may be restless, but don't give up. Your time is coming. And when your hour arrives, the door will open. When your hour is reached, the anointing will flow. When your time comes, what has blocked your way will make your way.

When your time comes, no devil, demon, distraction, disappointment, or detour will be able to hold you back. Just watch, work, and wait for your time. The future belongs to those who are prepared to take advantage of it.

God wants us to live balanced lives. One of the most common problems that I battle in myself and that I see in other people is the problem of imbalance. I'm not talking about just in people who have no acknowledged relationship with God; I'm talking about saved, sanctified, tongues-speaking, faith-walking, Spirit-filled believers: our lives are often out of balance.

Imbalance is a malady, an illness, a disease that has many different symptoms, but the root cause is always the same. You can be imbalanced in anything: sleeping, eating, working, playing, exercising, talking, praying, shouting, and waiting—just about anything. You can be imbalanced in the way you use your time, in the way you function in relationships, in sex, in anything.

The problem is that most of us have a tendency to work on our public lives and let our private lives slide. We work on how we look, how we smile, how we talk, how we dress. But that private side that is so well hidden from the probing public, that side that few people know, is the side of our lives that we often neglect.

Howard Hendrix made the point on one occasion that many people's lives are like poor photographs: they are either overexposed or underdeveloped. I think that's true. A lot of lives are overexposed. Everybody sees us and knows us. We have all kinds of contacts and connections. We know how to network. We have a circle of friends. But our private lives are undeveloped.

One of my favorite songs sung by BeBe and CeCe Winans says,

> From miles away they judge from my expression,
> And it looks to them that nothing could be wrong.
> Everything right now in life is going my way,
> And I must admit I'm playing right along,
> But you know and I know.[1]

All too often, we are overexposed and underdeveloped. And when our personal lives, our private lives, are not properly developed, when we're out of balance, it's only a matter of time before two things start to happen.

First, we become *frustrated*. Have you ever seen a clown at the circus trying to balance dishes on top of tall, skinny poles? He spins a dish until it is twirling perfectly on top of the first pole, and he gets everything in balance. Then he takes another dish and starts that one twirling on another pole, then another, and another, continuing the cycle.

The problem is that when he gets to the eighth or ninth pole, the first and second poles with dishes spinning on them start to slow down. The dishes begin to tilt and look as though they are going to fall off. So the man has to run back quickly and get the first dish spinning again. Then he has to run to numbers three and four and keep those dishes spinning. It's a never-ending cycle. If the truth were told, a lot of us live our lives that way. We're trying to keep numerous different plates spinning on top of the poles of our lives: our attention is constantly diverted from our priorities, to our pressures, to our positions, to our privileges, to our possessions, and so on.

Just when we get one area going, another one starts to slow down. We have to be here and there, do-

**Frustration is a result of imbalance in your life.**

ing this and that. We work on this area, then that area, a little over here, and a little over there. No matter how fast we move, though, or how hard we work, our efforts are never enough. After a while, frustration sets in. Just about the time you get one thing in balance, another "plate" starts to fall off.

The second result of imbalance is *fatigue*. When our lives are out of balance, the inevitable result is fatigue. We become tired, really tired, sick and tired, then sick and tired of being sick and tired. We're just plain worn out. Have you ever been worn out? Anyone who has ever bought a new set of tires knows that the tires need to be balanced. If they are not balanced, you're going to have a bumpy ride. There's going to be vibration. Your vehicle won't handle the shocks in the road as well.

If the tires on your car are imbalanced, eventually they will rub in the wrong place. You'll get a bulge or a bald spot. If you're not careful, you'll have a blowout. And that's what happens in our lives. If the tires of our lives are imbalanced, instead of rolling smoothly along the road, we'll be wobbling.

The faster we go, the more we'll wobble. With all that vibrating and wobbling going on, it's inevitable that we're going to be rubbed the wrong way. If we keep getting rubbed the wrong way, eventually we're going to blow up or just blow out. Tires blow out, but people burn out when their lives are out of balance. Just as a tire that is out of balance wears the wrong way, lives that are out of balance cause us to wear out prematurely.

We can't go the distance because there's too much wobbling in our lives. We're worn out. What do you do for wobbling? You get balanced. Does the Bible have anything to say about that? Definitely. In Luke 2:52, we are given a glimpse of the early life of Jesus. Jesus lived a balanced life.

The Bible says of Him, *"And Jesus increased in wisdom and stature, and in favor with God and men."* Jesus grew in wisdom. He grew intellectually, physically, spiritually, and socially. He was a perfect representation of balanced humanity.

I want you to look at five areas of your life that need to be examined and kept in balance. This is the moment for you to pull your life together. Stop wobbling down the road of life, headed for a blowout. Seek balance in your life. If your personal, private life is out of balance, it affects everything else. First, build into your life:

## Mental Balance

Romans 12:2 says, *"Do not be conformed to this world."* The *Phillips Modern English* translation says, *"Don't let the world around you squeeze you into its own mould."* The verse continues, *"But be transformed...."* How? By your willpower? No. By working real hard? No. *"Be transformed by the renewing of your mind."* What we think about affects our lives. So the first step we must take to build a balanced life is to build mental balance into our days and our weeks. We must intentionally pursue intellectual growth and a renewed mind. The Scriptures teach that as a man *"thinks in his heart, so is he"* (Prov. 23:7). We need balance.

How do you build mental balance? First, by stretching your mind.

**If you do not use your mind, you will probably lose your mind.**

This means setting intellectual growth as a goal, plotting a pattern of lifelong learning, seeking to know what you don't know, endeavoring to enlarge and use your mind, and keeping your brain stimulated. What you don't use, you slowly lose. And I don't know how you feel or what you think, but I want to have as much of "me" working at full capacity for as long as I can.

Mental balance is built by stretching our minds and by screening our input. Stretching and screening. In pursuit of balance, we must screen the things that come into our minds. We cannot afford to permit anything and everything to come into our thought lives indiscriminately. You know the saying, Garbage in, garbage out.

Trash accumulates. It's a part of life. That's why if you are a good housekeeper, you line your trash cans with plastic, and you empty them regularly. If you don't line your cans, although the trash is gone, the residue will remain. If you don't empty the cans regularly, they will smell up the place. Balance is achieved mentally by stretching our minds and screening the contents. That means that you must choose what you're going to think about. Don't let your mind be a dumpster.

Jesus said, *"You will know the truth, and the truth will set you free"* (John 8:32 NIV). As we fill our minds with truth, we will find freedom in our lifestyles. Freedom comes by having the right kind of thoughts. True thoughts, honest thoughts, and loving thoughts form the basis for mental balance. We are told in Scripture to think about things that are virtuous and good. (See Philippians 4:8.)

## Physical Balance

We must also build into our lives physical balance. First Corinthians 6:19–20 says,

> Do you not know that your body is the temple of the Holy Spirit who is in you, whom you have from God, and you are not your own? For you were bought at a price; therefore glorify God in your body and in your spirit, which are God's.

May I ask you a question: "Do you glorify God in your body?" We all need physical balance. When we don't take care of our bodies, it affects everything else. If you don't take of your body, it won't take care of you. Our bodies are the vehicles we've been given for time travel, and they require proper care. If you burn the candle at both ends, you will only get to the middle quicker. We must work to maintain physical balance. You can translate that statement into: Get in shape. Perhaps you think, "I could never get in shape. I'm too old. You can't teach an old dog new tricks." It's never too late to change!

Dr. Kenneth Cooper, who invented aerobics, tells the story of a lady who came to him complaining of back pain. It was so terrible that she could not walk more than seventy-five feet without having to sit down.

She was stooped over and couldn't stand up. As a result of her condition, her social life was nil. When she came to Dr. Cooper, he advised her to have back surgery, but she said, "No." She wanted to try something else, so she began to walk on a treadmill.

She found that when she put the treadmill at a certain angle, she could walk without being in pain for about twenty-five seconds. She began to walk on the treadmill several times a day. Soon she found she could lower the treadmill more and more. Finally, she was walking on a flat surface without any pain for the first time in months.

Next, she added some slow jogging to her walking routine. Eventually, she began jogging continuously from three to five miles to ten miles at each outing. Today, this woman has run nine marathons, with her best time being three hours and three minutes. That's a great time for a woman or man of any age. If you want to, you can change.

## Emotional Balance

We must also have *emotional balance.* Galatians 5:22–23 provides us with a clear portrait of an emotionally balanced person. This text says, *"The fruit of the Spirit is love, joy, peace, longsuffering, kindness, goodness, faithfulness, gentleness, self-control."* Those nine qualities are the qualities of emotional stability. When you're emotionally stable, you are not blown away by a crisis. The fruit of the Spirit paints a picture of Jesus. Jesus is *"love, joy, peace, longsuffering, kindness, goodness, faithfulness, gentleness, self-control"*— all wrapped up into one. What about you?

Are you an emotionally balanced person? Do you have a tendency to worry constantly? Are you a moody person? Do you let your moods go up and down? Are you mastered by your moods rather than managing your moods? Do you get depressed?

I think emotional balance is a combination of confidence and contentment. You're confident and contented because your trust is in God. That means acknowledging that in your best moments, you still have faults, flaws, and weaknesses, but you trust God to work in you and through you despite your failures.

Let me illustrate with a familiar story by an unknown author. A water bearer in India had two large water pots. They hung on either end of a pole that he carried across the back of his neck. One of the pots had a crack in it, while the other pot was perfect. Daily, the water bearer would carry the two pots down the long trail to get water from a stream. Each day, the perfect pot would deliver a full pot, while the cracked pot would contribute only a half-filled jar of water.

Of course, the perfect pot was proud of its achievements, but the cracked pot was ashamed of its flaw. It was miserable because it could do only half of what it was intended to do. After two years of bitter failure, the cracked pot spoke to the bearer and said, "I am so ashamed of myself."

The water bearer said, "Why? What are you ashamed of?"

The pot answered, "Because I am so flawed. You do all of this work, but you don't get the full value from your efforts."

The water bearer did not speak at first. Instead, he picked up the pots and began walking back to his master's house. The cracked pot was leaking and feeling bad, when suddenly, the water bearer said to it, "Look down. What do you see?"

The cracked pot answered, "I see rows of flowers."

He asked the pot, "On both sides of the road?"

The pot answered, "No, only on my side."

The water bearer said, "That's the point. I have always known about your flaw, so I made provision for it. I planted seeds on your side of the path. Every day as we walked back from the stream, you thought you were leaking, when all the while you were watering. Without your being just the way you are, the master would not have the beautiful flowers that grace his home."[2]

Every one of us is a cracked pot, and God knows it. There's no use in posturing, posing, or pretending: we're cracked pots. However, if we trust God, if we look to Him, if we lean on Him, God can take our flaws and grow flowers. In our weakness, God will make us strong. What a basis for emotional stability in our lives!

A deep-seated awareness of God working in our lives provides us with contentment and confidence. We may be flawed, but God is still working in us. We may be cracked, but God is still working with us. We may appear to be leaking, but God is watering tomorrow's harvest.

## Social Balance

Fourth, we must work to build *social balance* into our lives. You can have nearly everything right in your life, but if your relationships are lousy, life stinks. You can be a millionaire, you can be popular, you can be well-known and successful, but if you are at odds with people, life is tough. You need emotional balance and social balance in your life. Success is meaningless if you don't have someone with whom to share it. We were created for relationships.

Romans 12:16 says, *"Live in harmony with one another"* (NIV). I looked up the word *balance* in Webster's dictionary. It says that balance is "when all of the parts are in harmony." When all of your relationships are in harmony, there is social balance. Romans 12:18 says, *"If it is possible, as much as depends on you, live peaceably with all men."* That's social balance. I can't impress on you enough the importance of this balance.

I read an article about fifteen hundred outstanding achievers from all walks of life. Researchers had studied them to try to identify any common denominators that would indicate the reasons behind these people's successes. Were there any characteristics among them that caused them to perform at such levels?

This research uncovered seven key factors, but the number one characteristic of the top achievers in the world is this: they lead a well-rounded life. They're balanced. High achievers are not extremists who spend all their time on one thing. That's a misconception. High performers are willing to work hard but within strict limits. For them, work is not everything.

In another study of top executives in ten major industries, the research found that these executives knew how to relax. They could leave their work at the office. They valued their relationships with close friends and their family life. They spent a healthy amount of time with their family and friends. They were balanced.

When any part of your life becomes all-important, then everything, including that part, begins to crumble. Balance is the key.

## Spiritual Balance

Finally, we must build *spiritual balance* into our lives. That's part of our personal lives, and it's critically important. Second Peter 3:18 says, *"Grow in the grace and knowledge of our Lord and Savior Jesus Christ."* As a Christian, you do two things: you grow in grace, and you grow in the knowledge of Jesus Christ. You have intellectual growth; you know about the contents of the Bible. Yet living out what you know about God helps you to grow in grace and develop godly character. It helps you to learn to enjoy a relationship with God on a daily basis.

A lot of people grow in knowledge. They know about God. They know the books of the Bible. They've memorized verses. They know who Nebuchadnezzar is. They know all about the Jebusites, the Amorites, and even the Hittites, but they don't grow in grace. We must build balance into our spiritual lives, and we can do that by concentrating on five actions: praying, studying, worshipping, fellowshipping, and serving.

First, we must *pray*. Proverbs 3:6 states, *"In all your ways acknowledge Him, and He shall direct your paths."* We must also *study*. Second Timothy 2:15 tells us, *"Study to show thyself approved unto God, a workman that needeth not to be ashamed"* (KJV). We need to *worship*. The Bible says, *"God is Spirit, and those who worship Him must worship in spirit and truth"* (John 4:24).

Building balance in our spiritual lives also means that we need to *fellowship*. Hebrews 10:24–25 says, *"Let us consider one another in order to stir up love and good works, not forsaking the assembling of ourselves together."* And we must *serve*. Find your gift. Find your ministry. Discover your purpose. Romans 12:6–8 says,

> *Having then gifts differing according to the grace that is given to us, let us use them: if prophecy, let us prophesy in proportion to our faith; or ministry, let us use it in our ministering; he who teaches, in teaching; he who exhorts, in exhortation; he who gives, with liberality; he who leads, with diligence; he who shows mercy, with cheerfulness.*

It's about balance. Finding and maintaining balance will revolutionize your spiritual life and help you to grow, to understand the things of God more clearly, to trust God, and to become more and more what He wants you to be.

How do you get started? Here are three suggestions from the Word of God on how to get started. Proverbs 14:8 declares, *"The wisdom of the prudent is to understand his way, but the folly of fools is deceit."* Wise people think about where they're headed. Fools deceive themselves. Proverbs 14:15 says, *"The simple believes every word, but the prudent considers well his steps."* How do you get started developing balance in your life?

## Step #1: Take Inventory

Look at your life and ask yourself, "Where am I in balance? Where am I out of balance?" Evaluate your life. Be honest. Keep it real. Do a self-examination. Have a spiritual, mental, emotional, physical, and social checkup. Examine your lifestyle. It's wise to analyze. Socrates said, "The unexamined life is not worth living." Edgar Guest said in a poem entitled, "Myself," "I have to live with myself, and so / I want to be fit for myself to know."

How do you avoid coming to the end of your life and saying, "If only I'd done...?" You do it by stopping in the middle of life— stop spinning the plates on the poles and look at your life. Evaluate it, and ask yourself, "Where am I out of balance? What's missing?"

Do you remember the story of the Prodigal Son that is told in Luke 15? The Prodigal went out and spent all his money. He had a good time with wine, women, and song, but he ran out of his inheritance. He ended up living in a pigsty, eating pigs' food. But in Luke 15:17, he came to the turning point. The text says, *"He came to his senses,"* and he said to himself, *"How many of my father's hired men have food to spare, and here I am starving to death!"* (NIV).

Have you done that? Have you come to your senses? Have you said, "I'm not going to waste the rest of my life. I'm going to make it count. I'm going to get my life in balance"? I want to challenge you to do a personal checkup. Ask yourself, "Am I mentally sharper than I was five years ago? If not, what am I going to do about it?

"Am I paying attention to my body? Is my body trying to tell me something? Am I getting enough sleep? Am I exercising? Am I eating right or just throwing anything that tastes good down the old trap? Am I going to do anything about it? Am I a workaholic, or do I take time off for physical restoration?"

How about your spiritual balance? Ask yourself, "Is my first reaction to a problem to pray or to panic? Do I acknowledge God *first,* or do I turn to God as a last resort? Do I take time for fellowship with God? Do I trust Him? Do I read the Bible on a regular basis? Am I choosing to grow spiritually?"

What about your emotions? Are you worrying a lot? Are you moody? Are you mastered by your emotions? Do you lose your temper at the slightest little thing? Are you irritable? Do you get depressed easily? Have you taken your "cracked pot" to God?

What about socially? Do you have anybody in your life whom you can count on as a genuine friend? Can anybody count on you as a true friend?

If you're really serious about getting your life in balance, I want to encourage you to ask your mate (if you're married) or your closest friend (if you're single) to help you to evaluate yourself. All of us have blind spots. We have stuff about us that we can't see. The Bible says that *"in the multitude of counselors there is safety"* (Prov. 11:14). So, when in doubt, check it out. Ask your trusted friends how they think you're doing—emotionally, physically, spiritually, mentally, and socially. Get several opinions. After you have taken inventory, move to the next step.

## Step #2: Write a Plan of Action

Often we plan every area of our lives except our personal lives. Balance does not come by accident. We have to work at it. It's not automatic. We must plan, set goals, and say specifically what we're going to do.

Ephesians 5:15–16 says, *"See then that you walk circumspectly, not as fools but as wise, redeeming the time."* Don't be foolish in the way you use your time. Be careful. Analyze your schedule. Make the most of every opportunity. How do you do that? By planning for it. By preparing for it. Then, when opportunity comes, you're ready for it. You develop a plan of action.

One of the things that helps us to build balance in our lives is habit. We are creatures of habit. It's not easy to let go of bad habits and establish good ones. We can't do it on our own. Willpower is not enough. We need more.

## Step #3: Let God Be Your Center

Just like a wheel has to have a hub, your life has to have something to center on. You will always be out of balance until you get something—one thing—upon which your life centers. You can center it on making money, but that will send you out of balance. You can center it on retiring and recreation, but that will throw you out of balance. Put God at the center.

In a wheel, all the power comes through at the point of the hub. Then it's distributed to the spokes that turn the wheel. Likewise, when God is at the center of your life, the power comes from Him. Under His control and direction, the power goes out to all the other areas and gives you balance.

That's why the Bible says, *"Seek first the kingdom of God and His righteousness"* (Matt. 6:33). Then all the other aspects of your life will be brought into focus—into balance. A person came to me recently and said, "I have a problem. My life is falling apart." How do you put back together a life that is falling apart? What holds it together? I asked the person, "Would you like to know the glue that would put your life together?"

Jesus is the glue of life. Colossians 1:15 says that Jesus *"is the image of the invisible God."* Even though we can't see glue, we know it's there holding things together. Jesus always has and always will be the One who can restore balance and order to your life. His Word says,

> *For by Him all things were created that are in heaven and that are on earth, visible and invisible, whether thrones or dominions or principalities or powers. All things were created through Him and for Him. He is before all things, and in Him all things consist.* (Col. 1:16–17)

If your life is falling apart, it's because Jesus Christ is not at the center. Christ holds all things together. Invite Him to be at the center, and watch Him put your life back together. Christ brings families, marriages, people, and even dreams together.

The benefits of a balanced life are tremendous: contentment, confidence, fewer aches and pains, more energy, no more wobbling. You will enjoy life more. You will be more mentally alert and more spiritually deep. You will be more emotionally stable. You will feel better physically. You will enjoy your friendships and relationships more. It all flows from balance. God can take your flaws and give you flowers.

**Put Jesus at the center of your life.**

Would you pray a prayer in your heart right now and ask Him to be the center of your life? Whether you've never done it before or this is the fiftieth time, would you ask Him to become the focal point of your life so that everything else will be brought into balance? If your life is falling apart, remember that He loves you, He wants to help you, and He's waiting on you.

### Prayer:

> Jesus Christ, please take the pieces of my life and put them back together. Lord, I thank You that You can

help me to live a balanced life. Thank You that the principles of balance are found in Your Word. I pray for a new joy, a new peace, and a new contentment as I strive to be all that You want me to be. Help me to become a balanced person. In Jesus' name, I pray. Amen.

# 10

# CONFRONT LIFE COURAGEOUSLY

No one wants to be called a coward. Cowardice is one of the most despised of all human characteristics. Most of us will do almost anything to avoid being called a coward.

In the neighborhood where I grew up, kids would dare you, then double dare you, then triple dare you. The ultimate was to be double-dog dared to do something. We would do all types of things—dumb things, stupid things, dangerous things, life-threatening things—all to avoid that dreaded word: *chicken.*

The entire world loves courageous people and despises the cowardly. In movies, often the bad guys are cowardly and the good guys are courageous. In families, fathers always want their wives and children to see them as being courageous because that's the stuff that heroes are made of. Usually when we think of courage, we think of people who perform death-defying acts or make heroic sacrifices.

Our heroes are usually firemen who bravely enter burning buildings and rescue little children, soldiers who fall on grenades to save their buddies, policemen in the line of fire who take a bullet to save someone else's life, astronauts who sacrifice their lives to further the cause of space exploration, and mothers and fathers who face untold difficulties to ensure that their children have a better life than they had. All of these are examples of courage.

It takes an enormous amount of courage just to face the ordinary challenges of daily life. It takes a lot of courage to try to do the right thing without wimping out. Every day of our lives, we're called upon to make choices. Every day those choices reveal whether we are cowardly or courageous.

It takes courage to believe that life can be better, to get ready for what you do not yet see, to make a difference in your world. You can change your world only if you are changed. We can embrace the future only if we are ready for the future. If we want to make a difference, we must be willing to be different. We have to be willing to have people say bad things about us, be criticized, be questioned, be joked about, be ridiculed, and be willing to go on anyway. Jesus said in John 16:33, *"In the world you will have tribulation."*

**It takes courage to change your life.**

Notice that troubles are not an option. *"You **will** [hardships are going to come your way, so don't be surprised] have tribulation; but be of good cheer, I have overcome the world"* (v. 33, emphasis added). Would you like to live more confidently, more courageously? I want to suggest three practical ways by which you can develop the ability to confront life courageously on a daily basis, without running into fiery buildings or jumping on grenades. We can develop courage in our lives every single day by owning up, standing up, and speaking up.

## Own Up

Take ownership of your life and everything in it. *Own up* to your sins, your struggles, and your successes. Now I intentionally chose the word *sins* because that's a word we love to avoid. We like to call it everything else. We no longer call lying, lying; we call it an "inoperative statement."

We do not call stealing, stealing; we call it "temporarily misplacing the property of another." We no longer call cursing, cursing;

we call it expressing our belief in the damnation of the wicked in a non-theological way. We like to call sin everything else—a blooper, a blunder, a character defect, a flaw, our temperament, an oversight, a lack of good judgment—everything except what it is. But Scripture is straightforward: sin is sin.

Sin encompasses the things we choose to do that bring pain to our lives. Romans 3:23 says, *"All have sinned."* Now we like to read it, "Y'all have sinned," but the Bible says, *"All have sinned."* First John 1:8 says, *"If we say that we have no sin, we deceive ourselves, and the truth is not in us."* In other words, when we claim perfection, the only person we are kidding is ourselves.

**S-I-N =
Self-inflicted
nonsense.**

The Bible says that the person who claims to be sinless is simply not being honest. He is deceiving his own inner being. He is not telling the truth. We all have sinned, but we hate to admit it. We are afraid other people will think less of us when we admit that we have failed, that we have made mistakes, that we have sinned and fallen short of God's standard.

Yet being able to be honest about your sin—to say, "I'm sorry. I was wrong," or "That was my fault. Please forgive me"—is what it means to *own up* to personal sin. To take personal responsibility for your sins is a mark of emotional and spiritual health.

There are grown men who have never been able to say, "I'm sorry. I was wrong." That's cowardly. Maybe some of you who are reading this book have never been able to utter those words. Some people have never been able to say, "I have sinned." We don't like to own up to our sins.

I read about a little girl and her older brother who went to Disneyland to one of those shops where they blow glass and crystal. The little girl picked up a figurine and dropped it, breaking it into a thousand pieces. Her brother took it like a man and ran out of the building.

The little girl, though, opened her purse, pulled out the only money she had, and, with great fear and trembling, walked up to the owner of the store. Offering him her five-dollar bill, she said, "Is this enough?" The man said, "It's okay. You can go."

Now that was an act of courage! I know adults who would never even think of owning up to what they have done. It takes courage to admit when you are wrong.

What are you afraid to own up to? What is it in your marriage that you haven't owned up to, and you keep blaming on your spouse or your kids? The Bible says in Proverbs 28:13, *"He who covers his sins will not prosper, but whoever confesses and forsakes them will have mercy."* There are some short-term gains to avoiding responsibility. You can wear a mask for a while, but in the long run, denial doesn't work.

This inability to own up to personal sin and responsibility is the great destroyer of marriages, relationships,

**Denial doesn't work in the long run.**

and careers. The inability to say, "It's my fault. I was wrong. Would you forgive me?" has ruined more marriages, families, churches, and businesses than you or I could possibly imagine. Let me raise a gender-specific question to the man reading this book, "If you're driving and get lost, will you admit it?" Not a chance.

We say stuff like, "I thought I'd take the scenic route!" Sisters, a lot of "macho posing" is really just fear in disguise. It's the fear of someone's discovering that we're imperfect, that we make mistakes, that we blow it every now and then. When it comes to admitting that we're wrong, a lot of macho posing is just moral cowardice.

People come up to me all the time and tell me things they'd never tell anybody else. When they start to unload their burdens, share their shame, or express their guilt, I admire them. Often they'll speak in a quivering voice. They may be trembling or even have tears in their eyes. It takes courage to own up to our sins and our struggles—to honestly face ourselves and admit that we have some things we need to work on.

In addition, we may not say it, but everybody has some type of struggle going on in his or her life and heart. Own up to your sin; own up to your struggles, because that sets you up to own up to your success.

People who make a lasting, permanent difference for good in the world do it out of personal authenticity. Fakes, phonies, and cons don't last. But the truth lasts. When you live with the truth in your life, saying, "These are my strengths, but these are my struggles. Praise God for my successes," it makes all the difference.

Until and unless we acknowledge both our sins and our struggles, we will never be able to fully appreciate our successes. We will miss the miracle that God is working in us and through us despite us. Paul could be honest about his strengths, and so he said, *"Follow my example, as I follow the example of Christ"* (1 Cor. 11:1 NIV), but that was because he was honest about his sins and his struggles. He said, *"Christ Jesus came into the world to save sinners, of whom I am chief"* (1 Tim. 1:15). He admitted, *"For the good that I will to do, I do not do; but the evil I will not to do, that I practice"* (Rom. 7:19). But Paul also said, *"I can do all things through Christ who strengthens me"* (Phil. 4:13). Courage is owning up to our sins, our struggles, and our successes.

## Stand Up

Stand up for the truth. Stand up to your trials. Stand up as your testimony. First Corinthians 16:13 says, *"Watch, stand fast in the faith, be brave, be strong."* Today, very few people are willing to stand up for the truth, for what is right. In a world where tolerance is valued more than truth, where people even doubt whether there is such a thing as right and wrong, many people are afraid to stand up for the truth. We are afraid that we will be labeled. But there is right, and there is wrong.

This past week, where you work, in your neighborhood, in your family, or somewhere in your life, you've seen something done that was wrong. You knew it was wrong, and you said nothing about it. You did nothing about it. You did not speak up, you did not point it out, and you did not confront it. You remained silent.

Perhaps you thought, "I know that's wrong, but who am I to judge? It's not my responsibility." But Ezekiel 3:18 says,

> *When I say to the wicked, "You shall surely die," and you give him no warning, nor speak to warn the wicked from his wicked way, to save his life, that same wicked man shall die in his iniquity; but his blood I will require at your hand.*

That's sobering. This verse teaches that if I know the truth, if I know what's right, if I see somebody messing up his life, and I say nothing about it, God is going to hold me responsible for failing to warn that person.

Who was responsible for the Jewish Holocaust? Hitler? Yes, but also everybody else who kept his or her mouth shut while it was happening. Who was responsible for the enslavement of Africans? Slave owners and traders? Yes, but also everybody who stood by and did nothing about it. Who was responsible for the segregation and bigotry that people of color suffered in this country? Racists? Yes, but also everyone who permitted it.

God says that when I know the truth but do nothing about it, I am not part of the solution; I am part of the problem. All of us know people, friends, family members, coworkers, or classmates who are destroying their lives because they're ignoring God and God's purpose for their lives.

Most of us probably know someone who's involved in substance abuse—be it drugs or alcohol. Many of us right now know people who are involved in extramarital affairs. It's destroying their marriages and destroying them. Many of us probably know somebody who's cheating, stealing from the company, or stealing from the government.

You may know someone who's stuck in an addiction and cannot get out of it, and you have said nothing about it. The excuse that we give for our cowardice is, "They seem to be doing okay. They seem to be happy. Who am I to judge? It's none of my business." However, Proverbs 14:13–14 says, *"Even in laughter the heart may ache, and joy may end in grief. The faithless will be fully repaid for their ways"* (NIV).

There will be times when *out* of love we, as people of faith, must care enough to confront *in* love. There must be a moment when we say to that friend, family member, spouse, parent, or child, "You're making a major mistake in your life. You're on the wrong path. I care too much to let you

**Love cares enough to confront.**

blow it. I'm not going to let you do that. Because I care about you, because I love you, I'm going to confront you and say that what you are doing is wrong."

If you see someone doing something wrong, and you do not compassionately yet courageously confront him about it, you're not much of a friend. Sometimes love is tough. Love cares enough to confront. True friends will say, "I'm not going to stand by on the sidelines and remain silent. I care too much about you. I care too much about this relationship. It may make you mad or offend you when I tell you this. It may put a strain on our relationship, but I care more about you than I do about what you think of me." That's love.

If I were to go home and see my house on fire and know that my family members were in the house asleep, nothing could keep me from running to their rescue. The press might call me a hero or courageous, the fire department might call me crazy, and others might call me different things; but when it comes down to the bottom line, love leaves no choice. It's not an option. I have to do it. I have to take a stand out of love.

You have to care enough to confront. Where do you get the courage to do that? Where do you get the courage to speak to that relative, friend, or coworker who's gone off the deep end or is heading that way, about to make the mistake of his or her life? Where do you get that courage?

Psalm 119:41–46 says,

> *Let Your mercies come also to me, O LORD; Your salvation according to Your word. So shall I have an answer for him who reproaches me, for I trust in Your word. And take not the word of truth utterly out of my mouth, for I have hoped in Your ordinances. So shall I keep Your law continually, forever and ever. And I will walk at liberty, for I seek Your precepts. I will speak of Your testimonies also before kings, and will not be ashamed.*

If I really love God with all my heart, and if I really love the truth, if I really love people, then those things are going to motivate me to take action rather than to sit in cowardly silence on the sidelines. When I see someone I care about making a mistake or going the wrong way, I am going to say something about it.

Stand up for the truth, and stand up to your trials. Problems and hardships will come. Into each life, some rain will fall. Your way will get dark. Your road will get rough. But when trials come, when difficulties arise, that's not the time to fall apart; that's the time to stand.

Stand up to your trials. Sometimes you cannot fix them. You cannot change your problems or wish or talk them away. Sometimes all you can do is stand, but stand anyway. Paul said, *"Having done all, to stand. Stand, therefore"* (Eph. 6:13–14). This is key. Peter said, *"Do not think it strange concerning the fiery trial which is to try you, as though some strange thing happened to you"* (1 Pet. 4:12). Jesus said, *"In the world you **will** have tribulation; but be of good cheer, I have overcome the world"* (John 16:33, emphasis added).

What's the point? Christ handled tribulation so that we can handle it. When trials come, don't knuckle under. Don't be shocked or overwhelmed. Stand up to your trials. Look them squarely in the face and accept them, analyze them (that means look them over, ponder them, think about them), acknowledge God in them (that for whatever reason God has permitted this to enter the equation that is my life), and then answer them.

Say to yourself, "This is rough, but it's not going to kill me. I'm too strong to let this take me out. I've come too far to give up now. I've handled tough stuff before. I've been in dark valleys before. C'mon, trouble. If you want me, you've got to take me because I don't give up that easily. If you want me down, you're going to have to knock me down, then knock me out, because as long as I can look up, I'm going to keep getting up." Stand up to your trials.

Stand up as your testimony. You don't have to talk your testimony. Just be. Let what you do speak for you, introduce you, and explain you. And when people see you standing up for truth, standing up in your trials, you will notice that they don't require an explanation.

They will be able to look at you and know that you have something, that you know Somebody, that you're tapped into a power source that enables you to do what you do. Alleluia! Praise God! It's your testimony. You didn't make it here on your own. As John Newton wrote,

> Thro' many dangers, toils and snares
> I have already come.
> 'Tis grace hath bro't me safe thus far,
> And grace will lead me home.[1]

# Speak Up

Target three things in your talk. Speak up *about your journey*. Speak up *about your joy*. Speak up *about Jesus*. Your journey is unique. Nobody will ever know what you've been through unless you tell it. Nobody will understand the joy you possess unless you testify about the hell you have come through. Speak up.

I can't tell your story, and you can't tell mine. We have to tell our own stories. Paul told Timothy, *"God did not give us a spirit of timidity, but a spirit of power, of love and of self-discipline. So do not be ashamed to testify about our Lord"* (2 Tim. 1:7–8 NIV).

Truth is not a hammer with which to beat people over the head. It's not a gun that you fire at people. It's not a club with which you hit them, and it's not a dagger with which you stab them. But it is a tool with which we can help people. Many of you are thinking, "Lance, I know I need to tell my friends, coworkers, and family members about Christ, but I'm no expert. I'm a brand-new believer. I don't know the Bible. I don't have any verses memorized. I'm no Bible scholar. I've never been to seminary. I don't know enough to tell people about Christ."

Do you know enough to say, "Jesus loves you, and God made you for a purpose. Jesus died on the cross for you to demonstrate God's love"? That's what people need to know. People don't need your knowledge; they need your love. You don't argue anybody into an abundant life. You express love for people, and you build a bridge of love from your heart to theirs. Then you let Jesus Christ walk across. You don't have to be a Bible scholar to do this. You just have to love people.

The Scriptures remind us that as people of faith, we are called to share the Gospel. It's our *profession*. In Romans 1:16, Paul wrote, *"I am not ashamed of the gospel of Christ, for it is the power of God to salvation for everyone who believes, for the Jew first and also for the Greek."* Keep that verse in front of you, because that's our role. We are called. It's our job to speak up about Jesus, and we must *prepare* to do it.

Nowhere do we ever see that it's easy. Some effort is involved here. You have to listen. You have to read the Scriptures. You have to be in a small group where people can hold you accountable for the witness that you present by your everyday life. That means *practice*. That's how we learn to witness. We practice. Try it. It takes planning. That means forming a target list in your mind of people who need to know Christ. Invite those people on your list to come to church with you.

Have you ever regretted sharing the love of the Lord with anyone? Have you ever regretted extending the invitation to come to church? You never fail in this effort when you try. Sometimes there will be a knockdown or a setback, but Jeremiah 1:17–19 says,

> *"Therefore prepare yourself and arise, and speak to them all that I command you. Do not be dismayed before their faces, lest I dismay you before them. For behold, I have made you this day a fortified city and an iron pillar, and bronze walls against the whole land; against the kings of Judah, against its princes, against its priests, and against the people of the land. They will fight against you, but they shall not prevail against you. For I am with you," says the LORD, "to deliver you."*

That's the *promise*.

God wants to use you in this world right now, and He will—if you're willing to own up, stand up, and speak up. You know what to do. These principles are not new to most of you. The real issue is where you are going to get the courage to stand up and speak up when you need to. Here are four steps that will help to boost your courage and stoke the fires of your confidence, so that you can be a world-changer. What do you do?

## Step #1: Go Public

Let others know that you believe in God. One of the strongest public confessions of faith is deciding to be baptized. Baptism is your "coming-out party." Baptism represents that moment when you stop being a secret agent disciple and make your stand. When people are baptized, it's a statement to the world that declares, "I'm stepping across the line. I'm in the family of faith. I've joined the army of hope. I'm in the fold. I am not ashamed to tell the world that I am a follower of Jesus Christ."

A little boy who wanted to be baptized asked his mom, "When can I get advertised?" I love that story because fundamentally that's what baptism is: baptism is an advertisement for Jesus. Baptism is a personal declaration that says, "I'm not covering up. I'm not a coward. I'm not worried about anybody knowing this. I want the whole world to know that I'm a Christian, and I'm going to declare it in a very public act."

Few things are more public than baptism. When Jesus went down to the Jordan River to be baptized, it was a very public act. In Galatians 3:27, Paul said to the believers at Galatia, *"For all of you who were baptized into Christ have clothed yourselves with Christ"* (NIV). In other words, your baptism in Christ is not just washing you up for a fresh start. It also involves dressing you in an adult faith wardrobe of Christ's life. Have you made your confession of faith? Can I encourage you today to come out of hiding, step across the line, and go public? Take that step.

## Step #2: Pray for Boldness

Ask God for courage. Even the apostle Paul did this. He said, *"Pray also for me, that whenever I open my mouth, words may be given me so that I will fearlessly make known the mystery of the gospel, for which I am an ambassador in chains. Pray that I may declare it fearlessly, as I should"* (Eph. 6:19–20 NIV). Ask God for courage. Pray for boldness.

### Expect God to Use You

Perhaps today you might want to print the prayer below on a little card, put it on your desk at work, the visor in your car, or on your refrigerator door. Whisper this prayer daily to God:

> I expect and hope that I will have the courage now, as always, to show the greatness of God during my life here on earth.

## Confront Life Courageously

God works in your life when you show faith. You expect the courage to be there, and it will be there. Courage is not the absence of fear. Courage is doing the right thing in spite of your fear. Courage is not the absence of anxiety.

You're going to have anxiety when you talk to people about critical issues in their lives. It's natural to be nervous. Courage is moving ahead in spite of your nervousness, doing the right thing because you love God, people, and truth. In fact, if you don't feel any nervousness or fear, then it's not an act of courage, because you only need courage when you are afraid.

Courage on our part pleases God. In the Old Testament book of Joshua, God says to the aspiring young leader, *"Be strong and of good courage; do not be afraid, nor be dismayed, for the* LORD *your God is with you wherever you go"* (Josh. 1:9). Circle *"with you."* Go public, pray for boldness, and expect God to use you.

## Remember the End of the Story

It's easy to become discouraged as we struggle with the challenges of life. Discouragement is the opposite of courage. Notice the spelling: "dis-courage." When we lose our courage, we become "dis-couraged." However, as we take time to remember the end of the story, we find tremendous reasons to be "en-couraged." In the last chapter of the Bible, we are reminded of this: in the end, we win!

We may lose a few battles, but the outcome is fixed: we win. James 5:8 says, *"Take courage, for the coming of the Lord is near"* (TLB). Job said, *"You will have courage because you will have hope"* (Job 11:18 TLB). Don't ever be intimidated by someone who doubts God, despite what training and education he or she may possess. The Bible says, *"The fool has said in his heart, 'There is no God'"* (Ps. 14:1). It does not matter if a person has many degrees. People may address that person as "doctor," but if he or she says there is no God, the Scriptures call that person *"a fool."*

When I was in college, I used to hear people say these things all the time: "Religion is for weak people"; "God is a crutch for spineless wimps"; and "Christianity is for cowards." These statements couldn't be more wrong. It takes enormous courage to become a Christian. You have to own up to your sin and struggle. You have to repent, and that takes courage. You have to commit your life to Christ, and that takes courage.

It takes courage to be ethical in the marketplace. It takes courage to be honest, even when it costs you personally. It takes courage to minister. It takes courage to share your faith with an unbeliever. It takes courage to tithe. It takes courage to stand up for the truth, stand up to your trials, and stand up as your testimony. It takes no courage to blend in with the culture.

> **Cowards follow the crowd; the courageous follow Christ.**

Do you have enough courage to step across the line? Do you have enough courage to publicly profess your faith in Christ, first by being baptized, then by standing up for Him at your workplace? Are you willing to take your Bible, lay it on your desk, and let people know in love where you stand? Do you have the courage to do that?

My challenge to you today is this: dare to make a difference by daring to be different. Care more about what God thinks than what other people think. You need to live only for an audience of One—Jesus Christ. Great people never follow the crowd. Never. They take the "road less traveled."

Let me ask you a very personal question. Whom do you need to talk to about Jesus Christ? Your neighbor? Your coworker? Your family member? I want you to do something courageous. Pray that God will give you the opportunity to share the love of Jesus with a person you know. Then trust God to help you to do it. Do something courageous today.

## Prayer:

God, I don't want to be a coward. Forgive me for those times when I have been silent and I should have spoken up. I want to own up to my sin, my struggle, and my success. I want You to be in charge of every area of my life. I don't want to be a closet Christian anymore. Give me the courage to stand up for the truth, to stand up to my trials, and to stand up as my testimony. Then help me to speak up about my journey, my joy, and my Jesus. In Your name, I pray. Amen.

# 11

# DEEPEN YOUR DISCIPLINE

I n a letter to the early church at Corinth, the apostle Paul asked this question, *"Do you not know that those who run in a race all run, but one receives the prize?"* (1 Cor. 9:24). Then he went on to make this statement:

> *Run in such a way that you may obtain it. And everyone who competes for the prize is temperate in all things. Now they do it to obtain a perishable crown, but we for an imperishable crown. Therefore I run thus: not with uncertainty. Thus I fight: not as one who beats the air. But I discipline my body and bring it into subjection, lest, when I have preached to others, I myself should become disqualified.* (1 Cor. 9:24–27)

The *New International Version* says, *"Everyone who competes in the games goes into strict training. They do it to get a crown that will not last; but we do it to get a crown that will last forever"* (v. 25). What's the point? By God's grace, we must build into ourselves a sense of personal discipline. Every great achiever shares one common denominator: a growing sense of personal discipline. Paul was an extremely disciplined person. He had tremendous self-control. Paul said, in essence, "I want to be a success. I am running not just to compete, but also to win. I'm in it to win it."

Discipline is not easy, but it is effective. Discipline is not a popular subject today. Practical principles of prayer, perseverance, patience, and productivity have fallen into disrepute in our time. Our public and personal lives are plagued by the personal pursuit of pleasure. The prevailing ideology of our day seems to be, "Don't think about it. Don't contemplate the long-term consequences. Don't focus on the outcome. If it feels good, do it. If it doesn't feel good, dump it." Tragically, too often, our focus is fixed on what's fun. If it's fun, find it. If it's not fun, forget it. Anything that is unpleasant should be avoided at all costs. We do not like good, old-fashioned discipline.

I saw a recent Milo and Otis cartoon where Otis asked Milo to be his diet coach. Milo agreed and suggested that he try eating less and exercising more. Otis responded that he didn't want to do anything like that. He wanted a diet that would allow him to eat as much as he wanted, whenever he wanted. Milo suggested that Otis would have to submit to having his stomach surgically reduced. He explained that it would involve a hospitalization and a couple of weeks of recovery. Otis complained that he didn't want anything as drastic as that. He just wanted to eat whatever he wanted and not gain weight.

**Discipline is the key to achievement.**

Too many of us want any medication except a strong dose of discipline. We want wealth without work, success without sacrifice, a great body without exercise, spirituality without struggle, power without prayer, friendship without fellowship, blessings without burdens, roses without rain, and a crown without a cross.

The Scriptures teach us that discipline is the key to personal achievement. There will be divine interventions. There will be divine interruptions. There will be miraculous serendipities. However, by and large, throughout the incredible odysseys that are our lives, your blessing and my blessing, your miracle and my miracle, your deliverance and my deliverance will come on the tail end of some perfected discipline that we have met, mastered, and maintained.

If I pray for strong teeth, when I get off my knees, I have to practice the discipline of brushing, flossing, and eliminating sugar from my diet. If I pray for weight loss, when I get off my knees, I have to practice the discipline of diet and exercise. If I pray for a better financial situation, when I get off my knees, I have to get a job, go to work, build a budget, pay my tithe, and discipline my desires.

One man wrote,

> I asked God for strength, that I might achieve.
> I was made weak, that I might learn humbly to obey.
> I asked for health, that I might do great things.
> I was given infirmity, that I might do better things.
> I asked for riches, that I might be happy.
> I was given poverty, that I might be wise.
> I asked for power, that I might have the praise of men.
> I was given weakness, that I might feel the need of God.
> I asked for all things, that I might enjoy life.
> I was given life, that I might enjoy all things.
> I got nothing I asked for—but everything I hoped for.
> Almost despite myself,
>     my unspoken prayers were answered.
> I am, among men, most richly blessed.[1]

Discipline is the key to personal achievement. Here is a plan based on the Word of God for deepening the level of discipline in your life. First, the Scriptures teach us that personal discipline or self-control must be a priority.

While there are multiple areas where discipline must be our priority, I want to highlight six practices that will help you to make personal discipline the priority that it needs to be. If you want to live a successful, faithful life, you're going to have to work on these areas. You can use this outline as a checklist and evaluate your life and experience.

## Master Your Moods

Successful people are willing to do the things that most people are unwilling to do. One of the first disciplines we must meet and master in our effort to maximize our edge is to get a handle on our feelings. Are you a moody person? Do you live by your emotions? What percent of your decisions do you make because "you feel like it"? Are your actions based on your moods? Do you often say, "I didn't feel like it, so I didn't do it," or "I felt like it, so I did it"? We must master our moods. Proverb 25:28 in *The Living Bible* says, *"A man without self-control is as defenseless as a city with broken-down walls."*

Have you heard the story about the mother who went in to wake up her son? She said, "Son, get up, you have to get ready for church." He turned over and said, "Ma, I'm not going. I don't feel like it." She said, "You'd better get up. You're going to be late." He said, "But, Mom, I really don't feel like it. I'm not going to church because I don't like the people there, and they don't like me." His mother said, "Son, you've got to get up and go to church anyway." He said, "Why should I go?" She said, "I'm going to give you two very good reasons why you should go. First, you are fifty-three years old, and second, you're the pastor!"

Can you identify with that? Have you encountered something this past week that you needed to do, but really didn't feel like doing? We will never become successes by doing only what we feel like doing. In fact, multitudes of great things have been done by people who did not *feel* like doing them.

Discipline is doing what you *will*, not what you *feel*. That's worth remembering. The Scriptures teach that a person who has no self-control is defenseless. Without discipline, we are at the mercy of our moods. We're at their whim. We are helpless victims of our emotions. To deepen our discipline and achieve our greatest potential, we must master our moods.

## Watch Your Words

Proverbs 13:3 says, *"He who guards his lips guards his life, but he who speaks rashly will come to ruin"* (NIV). You can say the wrong thing at the wrong time and get into deep trouble! Proverbs 21:23 in *The Living Bible* says, *"Keep your mouth closed and you'll stay out of trouble."* That's good, plain advice. James 1:26 says, *"If anyone among you thinks he is religious, and does not bridle his tongue but deceives his own heart, this one's religion is useless."*

If I'm going to deepen my discipline, I must master my moods, then watch my words. One writer said, "The mouth is the grocer's friend, the dentist's fortune, the orator's pride, and the fool's trap." Many people have been "hung by the tongue," crucified by the very words they have spoken.

It is said that a hotheaded woman told John Wesley, "My talent is to speak my mind." Mr. Wesley said, "Sister, that is the one talent that God wouldn't care if you buried." If we wish to deepen our discipline, we must watch our words. This is hard to do. Be honest. Isn't it hard not to gossip?

One writer said, "Some secrets are worth keeping, others are too good to keep." I've heard that R. G. LeTourneau, owner of a large earthmoving equipment company, had a scraper known as "G." Somebody asked one of the salesmen what the "G" stood for. The salesman said, "It stands for gossip, because like gossip, this machine moves a lot of dirt, and it moves it fast."

> An unrestrained tongue is a sign of immaturity.

Watch your words. Discipline your speech. Work at it. If you can't say anything good, don't say anything at all.

## Restrain Your Actions

Proverbs 19:11 says, *"A wise man restrains his anger and overlooks insults. This is to his credit"* (TLB). Now be honest. Have you ever had somebody do you wrong, and you really wanted to get even with him? Let's go a step further. Do you find it easy to fly off the handle or to lose your temper?

I've heard some people say, "I had to give him a piece of my mind." You'd better stop giving away pieces of your mind; you need all you can get. A "short fuse," a person who cannot disagree with you without disliking you or discuss a hot subject without getting hot, has a discipline problem—his or her temper is not disciplined.

If I have to punch something because people don't see things my way, something is wrong with me—not them. If I have to cuss because people are not agreeing with my point of view, I have an undisciplined mind—not an unruly tongue. The tongue will say only what's already in the mind. The issue is discipline.

How much does it take to tick you off? One little thing? Or any and everything? Booker T. Washington said, "I will never allow another man to control my life by making me hate him."[2] When we say, "You make me mad!" what are we admitting? Who's in control of us? Somebody else. Someone else is in control of our attitudes. He or she is controlling the way we feel.

When I am angry because of you, that usually means that you are controlling me. Isn't it amazing that children learn this skill at a very early age? "I may be small, and I may not be as powerful, but if I can make Mommy mad, guess who's in control?" A disciplined person restrains his reactions. Second Timothy 4:5 teaches, *"Keep your head in all situations"* (NIV). Disciplined people choose to act rather than react, so they are not controlled by circumstances.

Proverbs 16:32 says, *"He who is slow to anger is better than the mighty, and he who rules his spirit than he who takes a city."* It's better to have control of yourself than it is to control an entire city. If you want to be successful, deepen your discipline in these areas. Master your moods, watch your words, and restrain your reactions.

## Stick to Your Schedule

Some of us have to develop a schedule before we can stick to it. We're living accidentally, rather than intentionally. Ephesians 5:15–16 says, *"Be very careful, then, how you live—not as unwise but as wise, making the most of every opportunity"* (NIV). We all have the same amount of time. We all have 168 hours a week. Why are some people more productive and effective than the rest of us? Personal discipline.

Discipline is demonstrated by setting a schedule, then sticking to it. How well do you manage your time? We all must face these three facts of life: (1) To be a success in anything takes time; (2) We don't have time for everything, so we have to be selective; and (3) If we don't decide how we're going to spend our time, other people will decide for us. We must stick to our schedules with a due sense of responsibility.

## Manage Your Money

Proverbs 21:20 in *The Living Bible* says, *"The wise man saves for the future, but the foolish man spends whatever he gets."* What's the point? We will never know peace, contentment, or real success by living paycheck to paycheck. Discipline has to enter the equation here. Don't spend all you get.

In 1996, the average American saved 4.4 percent of his income, while the average Japanese saved 13.8 percent.[3] Why are we so bad at saving? Because we like to live now! We have to have it now, even if we have to charge our purchases! We act as if living within our means means using a credit card! When the going gets tough, the tough go shopping.

Recent statistics say that the average person is buying $1300 on credit for every $1000 he or she earns. That's what's called deficit spending. We're imitating the government! The problem is, the government is the only one who can get away with it because it *produces* the money! We don't. Learning to manage our money is an issue of discipline.

**Learn to live on a margin.**

Impulse buying reveals a lack of discipline. Impulse buying arises from the feeling that because I've seen it, I have to have it. That's a wonderful way to end up buying things you don't need...with money you don't have...to impress people you don't like...and folks who don't care. Let me ask you two hard questions: How disciplined are you with your money? Have you learned to manage your money?

Contrary to what the commercial says, you can't "have it all," but, if you are disciplined, you can enjoy what you have more. To deepen your discipline, you must master your moods, watch your words, restrain your reactions, stick to your schedule, and manage your money.

## Maintain Your Health

First Thessalonians 4:4 says, *"Each of you should learn to control his own body in a way that is holy and honorable"* (NIV). Our bodies need more exercise, more rest, and fewer calories. That takes discipline!

Proverbs 23:2 in the *New International Version* says, *"Put a knife to your throat if you are given to gluttony."* Let me give you a definition of a dieter: a dieter is someone who realizes that if he is not careful, what's on the table will end up on his seat.

Take care of your body, and your body will take care of you. Successful people are simply people willing to do things that unsuccessful people are unwilling to do. They have personal discipline. So how do you develop a plan of discipline? Look in the Book. Scripture not only points out the priority of personal discipline, but also gives us a plan.

## Admit Your Lack of Discipline

The first step in plotting, planning, and practicing a program of personal discipline is to admit your lack of discipline. Don't deny it. Quit rationalizing. Quit making excuses. Don't ignore it. Don't say things like, "I don't have a problem." "I don't have a temper." "I don't have a drinking problem." "I'm in good shape." "I'm in control." Quit ignoring the situation, and admit that you have a discipline problem. Confess that you have a habit you cannot break. Don't say, "I can stop any time I want to stop." Right! Why haven't you, then? Admit your lack of discipline.

I used to say, "That's just not the way I am. I've never been that way." Then I realized that it did not make any difference what I had been, only what I wanted to become. And in order to become, I had to deepen my discipline. Even Paul, who was a tremendously disciplined person, had to struggle with this issue. He said, *"For what I am doing, I do not understand. For what I will to do, that I do not practice; but what I hate, that I do"* (Rom. 7:15).

Does that sound familiar? Every one of us wants to be disciplined. We just go about it in the wrong way. We try two things that don't work.

## Willpower Alone Is Ineffective

"I'm going to *try*...." There's a psychological principle that says, What you resist, persists. The moment you say, "I'm going to stop..."; "I should..."; "I must..."; "I ought to...," you are going to procrastinate about that very thing. There is a part of us—call it the old nature, the carnal man, evil, who you used to be, your alter ego—that is full of rebellion. It says, "I don't want to do anything that I'm forced to do." It's human nature. Willpower doesn't work. How many of you are still keeping the resolutions you made on New Year's Day? How many of you even *remember* the resolutions you made then?

## Experience Is Not Enough

Stop looking for a onetime experience to zap you, change your life, and suddenly give you victory in every area in which you struggle. For several years, I experienced real defeat as I looked for a magical, onetime key that was going to change me and let me live in sinless perfection. I'd go to this revival and that revival, this church and that church, thinking, "Oh, I'm going to get a word. This is going to be the key." I went from one thing to the next, one book to the next, one tape to the next, when what I really needed was *discipline*. That was the problem. I lacked discipline.

## Believe That God Will Help You

Next, you must believe that God will help you. *"For it is God who works in you both to will and to do for His good pleasure"* (Phil. 2:13). First, notice that God gives you the *will*—that's the desire and the willpower. Then He gives you the *ability* to do what you need to do. What God asks you to do, He gives you the power to do. Faith is very important in learning self-control. Why? You have to expect God to help you. You have to stop saying, "That's just me! That's just the way I am!" or "I'll never be able to change."

You must believe that you can change. Why? Because we always act according to our beliefs. Our beliefs control our behaviors. Our commitments or our convictions control our conduct. The way I think determines the way I feel, and the way I feel determines the way I act. Instead of working on the symptoms and forcing myself to change, I need to change my thinking first. Change starts in your mind—in the way you think. You need to believe that God will help you. If you don't think you can change, then you can just forget it: you won't ever change.

## Claim a Promise from God's Word

This is the principle of positive reinforcement. Eliminate the negative, and put something positive in your mind. Instead of focusing on what you don't want, focus on what you do want. We always move toward what we focus on.

Can I give you an example? There's a hot sweet potato pie on the stove. You're saying to yourself, "I'm not going to eat it!" You're focusing on the very thing that you don't want to do. Get your mind off what you don't want to do, and get it on a promise from God, a positive statement that gives you something to hold on to.

The Bible says, *"For as he thinks in his heart, so is he"* (Prov. 23:7). Replace temptation with a positive promise. If you want to break a habit, here's a great promise: *"Fear not, for I am with you; be not dismayed, for I am your God. I will strengthen you, yes, I will help you, I will uphold you with My righteous right hand"* (Isa. 41:10).

Second Timothy 1:7 reminds us, *"God did not give us a spirit of timidity, but a spirit of power, of love and of self-discipline"* (NIV). God says, "I want to give you self-control." A fruit of the Spirit is self-control. (See Galatians 5:22–23.) It's not willpower; it's the fruit of the Spirit. Philippians 4:13 says, *"I can do all things through Christ who strengthens me."* Get a promise and begin to claim it in your life, because self-control starts with thought control.

## Decide in Advance

Proverbs 13:16 says, *"A wise man thinks ahead; a fool doesn't"* (TLB). Ephesians 6:13 says, *"Take up the whole armor of God, that you may be able to withstand in the evil day, and having done all, to stand."* When do you put on the armor? Now! Not when you're in the battle, not when you're tempted, but now. You put on the armor in advance of the battle. Decide in advance.

Self-control is a choice you make in advance of the time you need it. You make the commitment before your moods move you. Lately I've been struggling with my exercise program. Every day when I wake up, before I get out of bed, my body starts saying to me, "You really don't want to exercise today. You really don't feel well. You stayed up late last night. You're tired. You ache. You have a busy schedule. People are waiting on you. You don't want to do this." I find aches in places of my body where I didn't even know I had places.

Do you know what happens when I wait until I wake up in the morning to decide, "Am I going to run today?" I don't run. Discipline is talking back to your feelings. When my feelings say to me, "You don't want to run today! You're tired. You stayed up too late. You don't feel well. You ache. You have a busy schedule," it's discipline that enables me to do it anyway.

**The heart of discipline is to decide in advance.**

My goal is to be able to say at least five days a week, "You're exactly right, but it's not open for debate!" Don't ever argue with your feelings. Your feelings will win every time. The heart of discipline is to decide in advance. That's true of anything—reading the Bible, praying, giving your tithe, coming to worship, any area of your life.

Don't wait until you're at the party to decide, "Am I going to get high?" That's the wrong time. Don't wait until you're in the back seat of a car or sitting in a hotel room to decide, "What are my views about sex?" That's the wrong time. Decide in advance.

## Enlist Support

Find people who can and will check up on you and encourage you. Make yourself accountable. The Bible says in Ecclesiastes 4:9–10, *"Two are better than one, because they have a good reward for their labor. For if they fall, one will lift up his companion."* The Scriptures say: *"Admonish one another"* (Col. 3:16 NIV). *"Encourage each other"* (1 Thess. 4:18 NIV). *"Exhort one another daily"* (Heb. 3:13).

You can look other people in the eye and say, "I have a need. I have a problem," and people will share with you, walk with you through it, and pray for you. Even the Lone Ranger needed Tonto. And each of us needs somebody. God meant for us to be with others who can help, encourage, and support us. When we fall, they will lift us up. Enlist some support.

Find a friend in church and ask him or her to encourage you, pray for you, check up on you, and call you. It will help you to deepen your level of discipline. I have members of the church I serve who ask me, "How is your diet? How much water have you been drinking lately?" Often I want to say, "None of your business," but I don't because they are my support. We all need help and support from friends.

## Focus on the Reward

This is a very important principle. Moses was an example of a person who made tough decisions. He demonstrated discipline by choosing in advance and focusing on the reward. Hebrews 11:24–26 says,

> By faith Moses, when he became of age, refused to be called the son of Pharaoh's daughter, choosing rather to suffer affliction with the people of God than to enjoy the passing pleasures of sin, esteeming the reproach of Christ greater riches than the treasures in Egypt; for he looked to the reward.

As Moses grew and matured, he made choices. Circumstances didn't dictate his behavior. He didn't follow fickle feelings. He chose. First he *"refused"* to be known as the son of Pharaoh's daughter. He chose. He followed a negative with a positive. He chose *"to suffer affliction with the people of God."* Why would anybody do that?

Moses was the second in command in Egypt, with all the wealth, pleasure, and fame of the world concentrated there at that point in history. Yet he rejected all that pleasure, prosperity, and power to go live with a bunch of slaves who were at the worst stage in their history. Why? He regarded *"the reproach of Christ greater riches than the treasures in Egypt."* He made a priority decision. *"He looked to the reward."*

Moses left pleasure, power, and prosperity and went to lead a motley mob of slaves on a forty-year desert pilgrimage. He saw that the long-term reward was going to be greater than the short-term pleasure. Discipline requires delaying gratification and postponing pleasure. Delaying gratification is a process of scheduling

**Deny the lesser in order to gain the greater.**

the pain and pleasure of life in such a way as to enhance the pleasure by meeting the pain first and getting past it.

Do the tough thing first. Get the pain out of the way, so you can enjoy the pleasure. The key to discipline is to downplay the pain; maximize and emphasize the long-term reward.

It is the same principle our parents tried to teach us when we were growing up—do your homework first; then you can go out and play. Get the work out of the way. Why do you eat dessert last? It will spoil your appetite if you eat it first. You eat the things you need first. Apply that principle in life. Do the tough things up front. That will do a lot for your marriage. In the later years, you will reap the benefits. Work through those problems early in your marriage. Don't put them off.

Do the tough things first, and focus on the reward. What are the rewards of discipline? They are absolutely incredible. Practice financial discipline, and you will have good credit, greater cash flow, and more prosperity. Practice moral discipline, and the result will be a clear conscience, strong self-esteem, and no fear of skeletons in your closet. Practice physical discipline, and you will look better, feel good, and have more energy. On the average, you'll live longer. Practice spiritual discipline, and get connected to God. The discipline you develop now will determine the quality of your tomorrows.

Where do you need to develop more discipline? Self-control comes from letting God take control. And that's your choice. God's grace is available to each of us right now to enable us to develop and deepen our level of discipline. All we need to do is receive it.

## Prayer:

> Gracious God, so many of us today are in the grip of some self-defeating habit, yet the fruit that Your Spirit yields in us is self-control. Give us the courage to admit our struggles and turn ourselves over to You. Give us a promise to hold on to. In the name of Jesus, we pray. Amen.

# 12

# FOCUS YOUR FAITH

Our ability to recognize, receive, and rejoice in what God has done, is doing, and will do in our lives is based on our faith. God is alive, active, and able, but we won't recognize these truths and walk in their power without faith.

God has already released your blessing, requisitioned your miracle, and ratified your deliverance, but you won't be able to receive it without faith. God has been good to you, and He is blessing you right now. The best is yet to come, but you won't be able to rejoice if you don't have faith.

Faith is the key. Now everybody has faith, even the atheist. The only element that distinguishes us is the amount of faith we have and in whom or what we choose to place our faith. The point and purpose of this chapter is to encourage you to focus your faith on the One who is faithful, to trust in the One who is trustworthy, to rely on the One who is reliable. I want you to focus your faith on and in the almighty God.

Someone said, "Faith is to life what a mainspring is to a watch." It is indispensable. Another writer has described faith as the "oil that takes the friction out of living." I want to share with you some principles that could literally change your life. These truths are so dynamic and revolutionary that if you incorporate them into your everyday pattern, practice, and pilgrimage, you will never be the same again.

Would you like to have more faith? How do you get it? The Bible says in Romans 10:17, *"Consequently, faith comes from hearing the message, and the message is heard through the word of Christ"* (NIV). The Bible says we get faith through listening to the Word of God. As we look at Scriptures that illustrate and explain how positive faith can make a difference in your life, your faith will grow.

What is faith? What are the benefits of having faith in God? What will faith do for you? What difference can faith make in your life? The Bible uses the word *faith* or the word *believing* 485 times in the New Testament. That fact alone should tell us how important faith is. Consider these eight benefits of faith.

## Faith Determines What God Can Do in Your Life

In Matthew 9:29, Jesus said to a man seeking a miracle, *"According to your faith let it be to you."* That's revolutionary, but it's true. As free moral agents, God has given us the power to choose. That one principle can change your life: you get to choose. We get to choose how many blessings we will know and have and experience in our lives.

We get to choose how many answered prayers we will have. We get to choose how much God will work in our lives. God will work *"according to your faith."* There are over seven thousand promises in the Bible, and faith is the key that unlocks those promises. Faith determines what God can do in your life.

## Faith Can Solve Impossible Problems

Jesus said, *"If you have faith as a mustard seed,...nothing will be impossible for you"* (Matt. 17:20). Some of you are facing impossible situations right now. You really need this verse. Let this text speak to your heart. It doesn't take a lot of faith. When you put a little faith in a big God, you get incredible results.

178

## Faith Is the Key to Answered Prayer

*"Whatever things you ask when you pray, believe that you receive them, and you will have them"* (Mark 11:24). I used to pray like this: "Dear heavenly Father, if You're not too busy, and if You can afford it, please hear my prayer." But Jesus taught, "Believe that you receive it, and you will have it." Believe in advance. That's the key to answered prayer.

## Faith Is the Secret to Achievement

Jesus said, *"If you can believe, all things are possible to him who believes"* (Mark 9:23). Why is that statement true? It is true because faith turns dreams into reality. It gives you the confidence to move ahead. Goal-setting is a statement of faith. Wernher von Braun, the man who, among other accomplishments, designed the first ballistic missile and led the team that put the first American satellite in orbit, said that there has never been a single great achievement in history without faith. It's the secret to achievement. *"All things are possible to him who believes."*

## Faith Is the Basis for Miracles

Jesus said, *"He who believes in Me, the works that I do he will do also; and greater works than these he will do, because I go to My Father"* (John 14:12). That truth has to be one of the most amazing verses in the Bible. Are you doing *"greater works"* in your life than Jesus did in His life? You may feel as I do: I'm not doing half as great as Jesus did—let alone greater! And yet Jesus said, "My plan for you, Lance, as you trust in Me, as you believe in Me, as you act on what you believe, is that you would do greater works." Does God still work miracles? Every day! He does them through people and through prayer. Faith is the basis for miracles.

## Faith Is the Key to Partnership with God

In fact, the Scriptures teach that *"whatever is not from faith is sin"* (Rom. 14:23). That's pretty clear. If we would be partners *with* God, we must have faith *in* God. I don't know how much you blew it this week, but I know that I did. God expects us to depend on Him, and He will increase our faith as we ask Him to help us.

## Faith Is the Way to Please God

Hebrews 11:6 says, *"Without faith it is impossible to please Him."* Parents, how many of you are pleased when your children put their trust in you? God the Father is pleased when His children are confident in Him and rely on Him. Faith is the way to please God.

## Faith Produces Success in Life

First John 5:4 says, *"Whatever is born of God overcomes the world. And this is the victory that has overcome the world; our faith."* Faith gives us confidence. It neutralizes fear. It gives us the ability to press on. Can you imagine Moses and Aaron standing before the Red Sea? It's getting ready to part, and Moses turns to Aaron and says, "You first!"

Faith gives us the ability to move ahead in confidence. Confident expectation and execution produce the success we desire. Having read about those eight benefits, would you like to have more faith? Would you like to increase your faith?

Faith is absolutely indispensable, but what exactly is faith? We are called and challenged to live by faith, but if the truth were told, many of us lack a working definition of faith. Ask people, "What is faith?" and they'll answer, "It's trusting in God." Or they will quote Hebrews 11:1, *"Faith is the substance of things hoped for, the evidence of things not seen."*

That's good, but *how* do you trust God? How do you embrace the substance of what you hope for? How do you gain the assurance of what you haven't seen? How can you make faith practical? How can you apply faith to your life, marriage, job, and dreams?

Faith is such a significant concept. We simply cannot adequately describe it in one word or one definition. Faith is like a diamond.

It has many different facets to it, many different shapes, colors, and sides. I want to turn the diamond of faith, lift it up to the light, and show you eight different facets of faith. Practically speaking, what is faith?

## Faith Is Stretching Your Imagination

The Bible says in Ephesians 3:20 that God *"is able to do exceedingly abundantly above all that we ask or think."* God can achieve in us greater things than we can possibly imagine. God says, "I can outdo that! You haven't seen anything yet!"

In Genesis 15, we are given an effective example of this first principle: faith starts with stretching the imagination. Faith begins with an idea, a concept, a vision, a dream, a mental image, a picture.

**Faith always starts with an idea.**

God spoke to Abram one day and said, *"Do not be afraid, Abram. I am your shield, your exceedingly great reward"* (Gen. 15:1). Abram must have wondered how God could bless him because his only heir was his servant, Eliezer of Damascus. God said, "I can see I'm going to have to give you a picture." Genesis 15:1 says, *"After these things the word of the LORD came to Abram in a vision."* God told Abram that Eliezer would not be his heir; instead, He said, *"One who will come from your own body shall be your heir"* (v. 4). For Abram, that should have been hard to believe. He was well up in years, and he didn't even have a child. But God took Abram outside and said, *"'Look now toward heaven, and count the stars if you are able to number them.' And He said to him, 'So shall your descendants be'"* (v. 5).

Faith always begins with a picture, a mental image, a dream, a vision, or an idea. God says, "Here's something you can visualize." Every night when Abram walked outside, he looked up and said, "That's going to be the size of my family!" The entire Jewish nation came out of this man. Later God changed Abram's name to Abraham, for he would become *"a father of many nations"* (Gen. 17:4), and that would happen when Abraham was one hundred years old!

God starts by stretching our imaginations, by giving us a dream, a vision. What you can conceive and believe, you can achieve. Faith starts with stretching the imagination. Faith is visualizing the future in the present.

When I first came to Saint Paul's as pastor, I didn't have a clue as to what to do. God knew it, my wife Rose knew it, and I knew it. I knew I wanted to minister, but I wasn't sure how to go about it. I went to a weeklong conference at the Crystal Cathedral in Garden Grove, California. During my stay, I visited their ministry building called the Tower of Hope.

On the top floor of the Tower of Hope is the pastor's office; it's surrounded by glass on three sides and affectionately called, "The Eagle's Nest." I was inspired by the view, and one of the staffers said, "That's critical." "How so?" I asked. He smiled and answered, "Well, God told Abraham that He would give the land to him as far as he could see, and *what* you see is always determined by your location."

**What you see is determined by "where you be."**

If you're up high enough, mountains look like molehills, trees look like shrubs, and lakes look like tubs. I came back to Richmond, Virginia, with this prayer, "Lord, lift me up so that I can see Your vision for me." Faith begins by stretching our imaginations. That's how it all starts.

## Faith Is Taking the Initiative

In Mark 5, there is a story about a woman who had been sick for twelve years. She had an issue of blood. She *"had been subject to bleeding for twelve years"* (v. 25 NIV). That made her culturally and ceremonially unclean. She had no social life. She couldn't be out in a crowd. And one day she heard that Jesus was coming to town.

She said to herself, *"If only I may touch His clothes, I shall be made well"* (v. 28). So she took the initiative, went out into the crowd, and pressed and pushed her way through them until she got close enough to Jesus to reach out and touch the back of His robe. As a result, she was instantly healed. Jesus turned around and asked, *"Who touched My clothes?"* (v. 30). His disciples couldn't believe He was asking such a question. With so many people crowding around Him, He was bound to be touched by them.

Jesus ignored His disciples' lack of insight and turned to see the person who had touched Him. He might have said to them, "The person I'm talking about has been through a great ordeal. She has walked the floor alone at midnight, shedding tears all by herself. She has been stung by sickness, bitten by betrayal, hurt by heartache, and damaged by disappointment. This wasn't just someone who accidentally touched Me; this was someone who took the initiative and came because she was hurting and in need."

> **Jesus recognized the touch of faith.**

Finally, the woman stepped to the front of the crowd. She *"came and fell down before Him and told Him the whole truth"* (v. 33). And Jesus said, *"Daughter, your faith has made you well. Go in peace, and be healed of your affliction"* (v. 34). She took the initiative. She broke the rules. She went beyond the boundaries. She pressed ahead, got through the crowd, and was healed. Faith is stretching your imagination and taking the initiative.

## Faith Is Risking Failure

There is no faith without risk. Faith means stepping out into the unknown when you don't know what's there. The Bible says in 2 Corinthians 5:7, *"We walk by faith, not by sight."* That means we walk, looking with spiritual eyes, not with physical eyes. We look at things from God's point of view, not from man's point of view. That gets scary. Faith is letting go of your security and stepping out of your comfort zone. Faith is saying, "I'm going to face my fears. I'm going to risk failure. I'm going to take the dare."

When our kids were small, Rose and I used to take them to the circus every time it came to town. I was always amazed by the trapeze artists. One person swings out from one side, and another person swings out from the other side. Then there's the moment of truth.

Two things go through the trapeze artist's mind when he is out there swinging. First, he says, "If I'm going to grab onto the other person, I'm going to have to let go of this trapeze." There's that moment in time when he is hanging there, holding on to nothing, transferring from the security of the bar to the security of the other person's hands. He knows that he is going to have to let go of the security of one if he is going to grab hold of the security of the other. Second, he realizes, "I don't have all day to do it! I have to make the decision now."

If he waits until "next time," then every swing will take him further away from the one into whose hands he must leap. If he doesn't jump soon, the swing will come to a standstill. He will be stuck and have to start all over again. In short, there is no time for indecision. And just like those trapeze artists, you and I have to risk failure. You have to take the dare. Jump! Make the step.

**The turtle makes progress only when he sticks out his neck.**

I think about Jesus calling Peter to walk on water. Peter risked failure. He could have drowned. Here's an interesting point about that story: if you ever want to walk on water in your life, you have to get out of your boat. Remember, faith is risking failure.

Dr. Benjamin Carson, one of the world's preeminent neurosurgeons, in his book entitled, *The Big Picture: Getting Perspective on What's Really Important in Life,* describes how failure gives us the wisdom necessary to attain a better perspective.[1] If we use our failures wisely, we can move beyond fear and take the risk to invest our time, money, energy, and reputations in worthwhile pursuits.

Jewel Diamond Taylor, a dynamic motivational speaker, said, "What you strongly believe and expect, whether it is negative or positive, is your faith. Your faith or your fear is your B. S. (belief system). Don't allow your B. S. to keep you from financial freedom, success, a loving relationship, a healthier body, or more peace of mind."[2] Step past the risk, and see the reward.

## Faith Is Expecting the Best

In Matthew 9:29, Jesus said, *"According to your faith let it be to you."* Faith is positive expectation. You expect God to answer. You expect the solution to come through. You expect things to work out. You expect to be a success. You expect everything to fall into place. Expectations are faith.

Jewel Diamond Taylor writes that right now you and I are pregnant. We are expecting either painful or positive things to happen, depending on our belief systems. We have to be careful that we do not permit others' beliefs in fear, pain, limitation, and failure to impregnate us. She says, "Start talking, acting, believing, visualizing, praying, giving thanks, and preparing for positive outcomes."[3]

If you absorb the erroneous thinking of others, you will start expecting the worst and never reach your potential. Faith is positive expectation. Last week a friend was telling me about his favorite restaurant in New York City. I made up my mind that the next time I'm in that area, I'm going to eat at this restaurant. My expectation is, "The food will be really delicious."

**Prayer asks for rain, but faith gets out the umbrella.**

Do you know how I know? The way my friend talked about that restaurant raised my expectation level so high that I could probably be served puppy chow on a platter, and I'd really enjoy it. Know what I mean? It's expectation.

185

We tend to see what we expect to see. We hear what we expect to hear. We act the way we expect to act. We feel the way we expect to feel. We get what we expect. We set ourselves up for failure or success, for fulfillment or frustration—depending on our levels of faith. Faith is expecting the best.

I want to encourage you to become a glowing, godly optimist. I want you to be so confident in yourself and in God that you will go after Moby Dick in a rowboat and take some tartar sauce along! Faith is stretching, taking initiative, risking failure, and expecting the best. But we need to realize that sometimes the answer doesn't come immediately. Sometimes there's a delay. The healing doesn't happen, the miracle doesn't occur, or the answer doesn't come. What do you do when there's a delay?

## Faith Is Waiting for the Answer

Waiting is an evidence of faith. In Psalm 40:1, the psalmist said, *"I waited patiently for the LORD; and He inclined to me, and heard my cry."* That's an evidence of faith. How you respond to the waiting rooms of your life is an evidence of your faith. How long can you wait? That's a mark of maturity. Some people can't wait worth beans!

They have not learned the difference between "No" and "Not yet." If God says, "Not yet," they think that means that what they are praying for is not going to happen. Maturity is the ability to wait. Faith is waiting for the answer, realizing that sometimes the answer is delayed. One thing I'm learning is how important timing is throughout the odyssey of life. In God's plan, timing is crucial.

Many times my request may be for the right thing, but the timing is wrong. Don't get behind God, and don't get ahead of Him. Be right in God's time, because His timing is perfect in your job, your marriage, your education, your retirement, and every other area of your life. Whatever you are praying for, God has the answer in just the right time.

Look at the Scriptures and notice how many times people had to wait for God's answer. During the waiting time, God was preparing them. Think about the children of Israel in Egypt. How long did they wait for a deliverer to set them free from their slavery? Four hundred years!

Even when Moses came on the scene, they had to wait another eighty years. These desperate people had to wait forty years for him to grow up in Pharaoh's palace, then another forty years for him to go to the desert to be trained. At eighty years of age, Moses was finally ready to lead them out. God's timing is perfect!

How do you wait? What do you do while you're waiting? How do you let your faith grow while you're waiting for the answer to your problem? Faith is stretching your imagination, taking the initiative, risking a failure, expecting the best, and waiting for an answer.

## Faith Is Following the Instructions

Faith is following the instructions, even when they don't make sense, even when they don't seem logical or rational. It's following the instructions obediently. Hebrews 11:8 makes a beautiful statement about Abraham. It says, *"By faith Abraham obeyed when he was called to go out to the place which he would receive as an inheritance. And he went out, not knowing where he was going."* That's faith.

Imagine this scene: God comes to Abraham one day down at the office. He taps him on the shoulder and says, "Abraham, we're moving!" Abraham says, "Great! Where are we going?" God says, "You don't need to know." Abraham says, "How soon do we leave?" God says, "Right now!"

Abraham says, "What's it going to be like?" God says, "Milk and honey!" Abraham responds, "Great! That's really descriptive! How will I know when I get there?" God says, "I'll tell you." Abraham says, "How long is it going to take to get there?" God answers,

"Don't worry!" "Okay!" Abraham says. Then he goes home and tells his wife, "Honey! We're moving! Let's pack." That took faith. Abraham obeyed God and headed out, *"not knowing where he was going."* Faith is obedience. It's following the instructions.

Remember the story of Gideon in the Old Testament? Gideon started with an army of thirty-two thousand, but in following God's instructions, he was left with only three hundred soldiers to go to battle against ten thousand soldiers or more. God didn't want the Israelites to rely on their own strength. He wanted to show them how He could deliver them as they obeyed His commands.

God gave Gideon the plan he was to carry out. Gideon then told his men, "Here's what you're going to take into battle. I want everyone to take a torch, a pitcher, and a trumpet." That's standard army equipment, isn't it?

Gideon told the men to watch him and do what he did. The amazing thing is that Gideon followed God's instructions, and his men followed his. Gideon told them, *"When I blow the trumpet, I and all who are with me, then you also blow the trumpets on every side of the whole camp, and say, 'The sword of the LORD and of Gideon!'"* (Judg. 7:18). Then they were to break the pitchers so that the light of the torches would shine. The three hundred men must have seemed like thousands, and the whole Midianite army *"ran and cried out and fled"* (v. 21). The Israelites didn't have to lift their swords because, in the confusion, the Midianites fought each other!

Just what God said would happen did happen, even though the plan didn't seem to make sense. Has God ever asked you to do something that didn't make sense? If He does, don't ask questions; just do what He tells you to do! Faith is following God's instructions. Faith is obeying and trusting, even when you don't understand. Proverbs 3:5 says, *"Trust in the LORD with all your heart, and lean not on your own understanding."*

## Faith Is Being Persistent

Faith is keeping on keeping on. Faith is never giving up. Faith is continuing to persevere. The fact is, people of faith simply don't know how to quit. They never give up. They keep on keeping on. Inch by inch, they work at it.

Sometimes waiting is passive. But sometimes you're being persistent, and that's active. You're working, striving, continuing. You don't give up, even though you don't see the answer. Keep working at your marriage, keep working at your job, and keep believing that there's going to be a breakthrough. Don't give up.

Think about Noah. He was an amazing man. God said,

> *Make yourself an ark of gopherwood; make rooms in the ark, and cover it inside and outside with pitch....I Myself am bringing floodwaters on the earth, to destroy from under heaven all flesh in which is the breath of life; everything that is on the earth shall die.* (Gen. 6:14, 17)

An amazing thing about this story is that up to that point, it had never rained. There was a mist that came up from the ground and watered the earth. That's why they had never seen a rainbow before. It had never rained. Nobody knew what rain was.

Can you envision Noah building an ark in the middle of the desert, having no idea how God would get water to the boat or the boat to water? It took Noah 120 years. People said, "That guy's a crackpot. He's building this big ship in the middle of the desert." But Noah was persistent, and he persevered. Paul would later encourage the believers at Galatia in this way: *"Let us not grow weary while doing good, for in due season we shall reap if we do not lose heart"* (Gal. 6:9). Do not give in, and do not give up. Faith is being persistent.

## Faith Is Rebounding from Failure

Here's a fact of life: everybody fails. No one is perfect. We all make mistakes. The only people who never fail are those who never do anything. And even then, they have failed to try. Everybody fails. A successful person is not a person who's never failed. A successful person is a person who got up from the failure and went on. It's a person who continued, who moved from failure to failure without losing enthusiasm. Failure is never final unless you let it be final.

God says, *"Do not remember the former things, nor consider the things of old. Behold, I will do a new thing, now it shall spring forth; shall you not know it? I will even make a road in the wilderness and rivers in the desert"* (Isa. 43:18–19). He says, "I'm going to bring productivity where there has been barrenness. I'm going to bring success where there has been failure. I'm going to bring fulfillment where there has been frustration. I'm going to bring water in the middle of the desert. I'm going to take a useless life and turn it into a useful life." He says, "Forget the past. Don't dwell on it. I'm going to do a new thing." Rebound from failure.

The Bible has some very important principles on how to recover from failure. Some of us have fallen flat on our faces. But I want you to know, that's not as important as your response to the failure. Are you going to lie around and let it get you down? Or are you going to get up and do something about it?

Some of us are still reacting to a crisis that happened a while ago—a shameful problem from our past, a divorce, a bankruptcy, or a major embarrassment. Faith says, "I will not dwell on the past. I'm going on with the Lord. I will look at the future. I will see what God wants to do in my life. I will see what I can become—not what I have been or what I am, but what I can become."

**Faith refuses to have a pity party.**

Faith gives us access to the power of God. How do you break out of a pattern of procrastination, get out of a rut, take risks, expect the best, wait for the answer, follow instructions, keep on keeping on, rebound from a failure? Focus your faith on God.

When my oldest son, Lance, was small, we went to a toy store to buy a Fred Flintstone inflatable doll. He saw it advertised on television and just had to have one, so we made the trip and bought the doll. When we got the doll home, I blew it up and left Lance in his bedroom to play with it. He punched the doll really hard, and the doll rocked and bounced back up. He hit the doll again. It rocked and bounced back up. He hit it again and again, and every time, the doll rocked and bounced back up.

I came back later to find the doll standing in the middle of the floor and Lance sitting in the corner. I said, "What's the matter?" He said, "Nothing. I don't want him no more." I said, "Why not?" My son answered, "I hit him with my best punches, but he won't stay down. No matter how hard I hit him, he keeps getting up." That's what it means to have faith in God. That's what it means to be a child of God. No matter how hard you are hit, you may be rocked, but you keep getting back up.

## Prayer:

> Lord, some of us have been hit time and time again. We feel as if life has used its best punches on us. Help us to forget the past and look to You for our future. Strengthen our faith and our resolve to serve You. Use our pain to make us more sensitive to a hurting world. Thank You for never giving up on us. May we face each new day with gratitude and an expectant faith, excited to see what You are going to do in and through us. In Your name, Amen.

# 13

# HOLD ON TO HOPE

The entire epistle of Romans can be summarized in five words: *Sin*—which explains why we need to be saved and what the basic problem is in life; *Salvation*—which details how we become people of faith and are accepted into the family of God; *Sanctification*—which instructs us how to mature and "grow up" into our spirituality, becoming stronger, wiser, and better day by day; *Sovereignty*—which reminds us that God is in control; and *Suffering*.

Suffering is a fact of life, like it or not. Everybody experiences some form of suffering. Interestingly enough, the Scriptures never attempt to explain suffering. Seldom are we told the answer to the question, "Why is this happening to me?" There is something strange and mysterious about suffering that we simply cannot quite define or explain.

Yet our faith gives us hope and comfort as we struggle in, through, and with suffering throughout our lives. We don't know why so often "good" people struggle while the wicked appear to prosper, but it helps to have a faith that encourages us that *"those who sow in tears shall reap in joy"* (Ps. 126:5).

We don't know why trouble comes our way or why circumstances bring sorrow, but it helps to have a faith that reminds us, *"Weeping may endure for a night, but joy comes in the morning"* (Ps. 30:5).

We don't know why we have to *"walk through the valley of the shadow of death"* (Ps. 23:4), but it helps to have a faith that assures us that, even there, God is with us and will comfort us. (See verse 4.) Both *"goodness and mercy"* will follow us all the days of our lives (v. 6).

We don't have simple solutions or pat answers to the mystery of suffering, but the Scriptures give us comfort and hope as to how we can face suffering, go through it, and come out better people than we were before our encounter with trying ordeals.

In Romans 8, there are three key words: *hope, wait,* and *groan. Hope* is used six different times. In verse 20, we read, *"For the creation was subjected to futility, not willingly, but because of Him who subjected it in hope"* (emphasis added). Verses 24–25 read, *"For we were saved in this hope, but hope that is seen is not hope; for why does one still hope for what he sees? But if we hope for what we do not see, we eagerly wait for it with perseverance"* (emphasis added).

The word *wait* is used three different times. Verse 19 says, *"The creation waits in eager expectation for the sons of God to be revealed"* (NIV, emphasis added). Verse 23 reads, *"We wait eagerly,"* and verse 25 says, *"We wait for it patiently"* (NIV, emphasis added). When we suffer or when we're in pain, the hardest thing to do is to wait. Have you ever been in an emergency room, waiting for a doctor to arrive? You know how hard it is to wait under those circumstances.

The Scriptures teach us that, in suffering, when we're going through tough times, one of the things we need to learn how to do is to wait. Wait expectantly. In Greek, the word *wait* means "to scan the horizon, straining every nerve, straining your neck trying to see the dawn breaking." When we go through tough times, we need to have hope, and we need to wait.

A third key word in this passage is the word *groan,* which is used three times. When God first crafted and created the universe, it was perfect and good. However, when sin, alienation, and fragmentation entered the equation of life, this "good" world became a "groaning" world. Our separation from the Creator brought with it the consequences of decay, frustration, bondage, and death. Verse 22 says, *"We know that the whole creation **groans** and labors with birth pangs"* (emphasis added).

Here Paul compared the world that is waiting for God to come and turn things around with a woman in labor who is giving birth to her child. Until I took Lamaze classes with my wife, I didn't know the meaning of groaning. Having shared with Rose in the births of our children, I've heard some world-class groaning.

Paul said that this is what the world, the entire creation, is doing now. The world *"groans"* like a woman in labor. The creation is upset because things aren't going the way they ought to be going. Creation is waiting for the Creator to come back and make things right again. In the same way that the arrival of a baby makes a woman's labor worthwhile—gives her pain a purpose—the restoration, redemption, and renewal that God gives and will give makes all of the struggle worthwhile.

Creation *"groans,"* and in verse 23, Paul said, *"Even we ourselves **groan** within ourselves, eagerly waiting for the adoption, the redemption of our body"* (emphasis added). Creation groans, and we groan.

Have you ever felt as if you weren't making any progress spiritually? You were frustrated, feeling that you were going nowhere. You asked yourself, "How come I'm not getting any better? How come I still have the same hang-ups I had years ago? Why do I keep falling for the same old temptations? Why do I still have the same weaknesses? Why can't I get it all together?" You groan.

Where is God when you're hurting? Where is God when you're really going through tough times? Where is God when your pain is so deep that you don't even know how to pray or what to pray? Here's the short answer: God is with you. Verse 26 says, *"Likewise the Spirit also helps in our weaknesses. For we do not know what we should pray for as we ought, but the Spirit Himself makes intercession for us with **groanings** which cannot be uttered"* (emphasis added).

God knows what you're going through. He understands your pain and is with you.

That's our motivation for "Holding On to Hope." When you want to let go, when you want to give up, when you're really hurting, remember, God is with you. God will help you. You can make it through anything when God is at your side.

The Scriptures teach that there are at least five sources of suffering. We need to understand that. Yet the Scriptures remind us that even in our worst moments, there are reasons to hang on, to press through, to hold on to our hope. Where does suffering come from?

## Suffering Comes from Our Situation

We live in a fallen, broken world. The fact that you're on this planet means that you're going to experience suffering. Creation is upset. When God made the world, it was perfect. Yet sin brought suffering. God told Adam,

> *Because you have heeded the voice of your wife, and have eaten from the tree of which I commanded you, saying, "You shall not eat of it": Cursed is the ground for your sake; in toil you shall eat of it all the days of your life. Both thorns and thistles it shall bring forth for you, and you shall eat the herb of the field. In the sweat of your face you shall eat bread till you return to the ground, for out of it you were taken; for dust you are, and to dust you shall return.* (Gen. 3:17–19)

When Adam severed his fellowship with God, it had disastrous consequences. Ever since that moment, pollution, corruption, and decay have been ongoing parts of life. Prior to sin, there were no weeds, just flowers—no thorns, just roses. The air was clean, the water was clear, and the ozone was intact. But when humankind chose to turn away from God, chose separation from God, the result was imperfection, flaws, and failure.

This is a fallen world. Jesus said in John 16:33, *"In the world you will have tribulation."* You will have problems. They are inevitable. M. Scott Peck, in his book *The Road Less Traveled*, says that trying to avoid problems and the pain that accompanies them is at the root of all mental illness. Ignoring problems only leads to greater pain.[1] Problems are a part of life.

Sin takes its toll on us and on the world in which we live. Earthquakes, tornadoes, hurricanes, and typhoons weren't in the world when it was first formed. It was perfect. But the world was knocked off balance. By just living in the world, we are going to experience problems; so one of the reasons we suffer is our situation.

## Suffering Comes from Sin

Don't act like you don't know the word *sin*. Most of us are well acquainted with sin, or as Iyanla Vanzant would describe it, "Self-inflicted Nonsense."[2] It's the stuff we do to ourselves that brings pain and heartache. Romans 5:12 says, *"Therefore, just as through one man sin entered the world, and death through sin, and thus death spread to all men, because all sinned."*

When Adam, the quintessential representative of the human family, blew it, he wrecked human nature. Although we are all born with that same sinful human nature, we are each responsible for our own sin, because we have the freedom to choose between right and wrong.

We are all sinners without exception—by nature, by choice, and by habit. Yet, if we remain that way, we become sinners without excuse. Romans 6:23 says, *"The wages of sin is death, but the gift of God is eternal life in Christ Jesus our Lord."* When we blow it, when we refuse to live our lives God's way, it causes all kinds of problems.

For example, the world could support many more people right now, but people are dying of malnutrition all over the planet. Some are dying because of political choices and turmoil and some because of religious conflicts. Numbers 14:18 states the transgenerational effects of sin. The consequences of sin reach from one generation to the next, and we know that's true.

There are children today who have never taken drugs themselves, but they were born addicted because of their mothers' drug abuse. We inherit all types of things from our parents and our grandparents: behaviors, ideas, patterns. Some of what we inherited already has the stamp of failure, futility, frustration, and death on it. We suffer as a result of our own sins and the sins of our fathers.

## Suffering Comes from Self

In Galatians 6:7, Paul taught, *"Do not be deceived, God is not mocked; for whatever a man sows, that he will also reap."* Many of the problems I have experienced in life have been caused by me. The devil didn't make me do it. He may rejoice that I did it, but he didn't make me do it. I'm not a victim. I just messed up.

I blew the money. I made the mistake. I was out of control. I didn't think before I spoke. I let my temper run away with me. I'm too controlling. I'm manipulative. I'm inconsiderate. I told a lie. I took what didn't belong to me. I thought I could get away with it. I'm lazy. I procrastinate. I make excuses for myself. Sometimes I am my biggest problem.

Remember the cartoon where Pogo said, "We have met the enemy and he is us"?[3] The enemy is "self." We refuse to listen. We refuse to learn. We are determined to do it our way—right or wrong. We say in stubborn refusal, "It's my thing. I'll do what I want to do. I don't have to answer to you. I'm an adult." We do what we want to do, what we are big and bad enough to do. We commit the act, and we suffer the consequences.

Do we suffer because God is punishing us? No. Did the devil steal from us? No. We did it to ourselves. We reap what we sow. Sow good seed, and you will reap good seed. Sow bad seed, and you will reap bad seed. Suffering, struggling, and problems in our lives come as a result of living in a broken world. They come as a result of sin and as a consequence of decisions which we make that cause life to become difficult for us.

## Suffering Comes from Satan

Choose a name—evil, the devil, the demonic, the adversary; it doesn't matter, it all points to the same reality. Namely, something is loose in the world that works against God; against the people of God; and against all that is good, right, true, and holy. Some people have difficulty with this concept and deny the existence of evil.

People who deny the existence of the devil remind me of the story of a boxer who was really getting pounded in the ring. At the end of each round, he would stagger, bruised and bleeding, back to his corner. His trainer would tell him, "You're doing good. You're the champ. He didn't even lay a glove on you. He didn't touch you. He can't fight. He can't even hit you." Finally the fighter looked up and said, "Well, you'd better go out there with me because somebody is knocking my brains out."

We may not acknowledge it, but we're in a fight with something. First Peter 5:8–9 says it like this,

> *Be sober, be vigilant; because your adversary the devil walks about like a roaring lion, seeking whom he may devour. Resist him, steadfast in the faith, knowing that the same sufferings are experienced by your brotherhood in the world.*

The devil is busy. The devil causes problems, brings disease, promotes death, encourages depression, offers despair, rides on disappointment, and exploits discouragement. Those things are all part of the arsenal of evil. The enemy causes distress and despondency. Jesus said in John 10:10, *"The thief comes only to steal and kill and destroy"* (NIV).

## Suffering Comes as a Result of Your Salvation

The mere fact that you are a person of faith in a fallen world is going to cause problems. This world is not our home! This world is no friend of grace. First Peter 4:12–16 in the *New International Version* says,

> *Dear friends, do not be surprised at the painful trial you are suffering, as though something strange were happening to you. But rejoice that you participate in the sufferings of Christ, so that you may be overjoyed when his glory is revealed. If you are insulted because of the name of Christ, you are blessed, for the Spirit of glory and of God rests on you. If you suffer, it should not be as a murderer or thief or any other kind of criminal, or even as a meddler. However, if you suffer as a Christian, do not be ashamed, but praise God that you bear that name.*

For some strange reason, and in a mysterious way, God both permits and uses suffering in our lives to bring out of us what cannot be realized any other way.

Philippians 1:29 says, *"For to you it has been granted on behalf of Christ, not only to believe in Him, but also to suffer for His sake."* Hear that today. Paul said it was a privilege to suffer for the sake of what is right. When you do what's right, some people will be glad, some will be sad, and some will be mad. People disliked Jesus; they will also dislike you. They mistreated Jesus, and they will also mistreat you.

Hebrews 11:25 says that Moses chose to suffer *"with the people of God than to enjoy the passing pleasures of sin."* He chose to withstand pain rather than do something wrong. There is a phony assumption in our world today that says, "I deserve and ought to be guaranteed a life of continuous pleasure, with absolutely no pain," but the Scriptures do not teach that false idea.

They do teach that integrity is more important than comfort, commitment is more important than convenience, and character is more important than conversation. As a person of faith, as a child of God, I am to stand for what's right, do what's right, and pursue what's right, whether it's painful or not.

## Coping with Suffering

Here's the key to coping with suffering. Romans 8:18 says, *"I consider that the sufferings of this present time are not worthy to be compared with the glory which shall be revealed in us."* Circle the word *"consider."* This one word is the key to understanding how to make it when you're going through a problem. The word *"consider"* in the Greek literally means "to calculate."

It's the word from which we get our word *computer*. The text is teaching us that when we suffer, when we're going through difficult circumstances, we should calculate, consider, compute, analyze, check out, and seriously examine our sufferings in comparison with *"the glory which shall be revealed in us."* The key to suffering is the way we choose to see it.

If you take two people and put them in the same trying situation, it will make the one while it will break the other. What key element makes the difference? How they look at their trials. Having the right perspective is the key.

**The key to coping with problems is our perspective.**

The five ways that we have just examined that Scripture encourages us to see what is behind our suffering can give us hope to hang on. Often the problem is the way we view our problems. When we're in pain, we're usually pretty shortsighted. We say to ourselves, "I'm hurting. I'm not in the mood for long-range planning."

When you're in pain, what do you tend to look at? Your pain. That's all you see. That's all you feel. All you see is yourself. The biggest temptation when we are going through a problem is to focus on ourselves. Then we develop a myopic viewpoint that says, "I don't see anybody else. All I see is me." That's your problem. You have a limited vision. Push yourself to look beyond your pain, and know that you can hold on to hope. God will give you just what you need to make it.

Hope gives us the ability to move forward to where we cannot see. A famous American cardiologist said, "Hope is the medicine I use more than any other. Hope can cure nearly everything." So many people are infected with "give-up-itis." They have lost hope. What is it that makes us tough enough to survive suffering, to tackle tough problems, and to deal with dreadful difficulties?

In 2 Corinthians 4:16–18, Paul said that it is hope:

> *Therefore we do not lose heart. Even though our outward man is perishing, yet the inward man is being renewed day by day. For our light affliction, which is but for a moment, is working for us a far more exceeding and eternal weight of glory, while we do not look at the things which are seen, but at the things which are not seen. For the things which are seen are temporary, but the things which are not seen are eternal.*

## The things that are going to last are things you cannot see.

Our problem is that we tend to look at what's seen. Those things are not going to last anyway. Instead, we should look at the invisible things that will last forever. Second Corinthians 11:24–28 provides Paul's testimony on suffering. He said,

> *From the Jews five times I received forty stripes minus one. Three times I was beaten with rods; once I was stoned; three times I was shipwrecked; a night and a day I have been in the deep; in journeys often, in perils of waters, in perils of robbers, in perils of my own countrymen, in perils of the Gentiles, in perils in the city, in perils in the wilderness, in perils in the sea, in perils among false brethren; in weariness and toil, in sleeplessness often, in hunger and thirst, in fastings often, in cold and nakedness; besides the other things, what comes upon me daily: my deep concern for all the churches.*

And as he considered those traumas, he called them *"light affliction"* and looked toward the unseen eternal *"weight of glory"* (2 Cor. 4:17). That was his perspective.

James 1:2–3 says, *"Consider it pure joy, my brothers, whenever you face trials of many kinds, because you **know**…"* (NIV, emphasis added).

What is it that's going to help you make it through your problems? It's what you *know* that will help you to make it through. Romans 5:2 says, *"Through whom we have gained access by faith into this grace in which we now stand. And we rejoice in the hope of the glory of God. Not only so, but we also rejoice in our sufferings, because we **know**..."* (NIV, emphasis added).

How can I have a positive perspective in spite of my problems? I know something. I know Somebody. I am hooked up with heaven. I have a relationship with God. I can see past what I'm going through right now. I'm holding on to hope.

Let me give you five things to think about before you face trying circumstances. These truths will give you hope to hold on to when you suffer—not *if,* but *when.*

## Suffering Will Pass

Suffering has "come to pass," not to stay. Paul said, *"Our light and momentary troubles are achieving for us an eternal glory that far out-weighs them all"* (2 Cor. 4:17 NIV). The sufferings we experience now are nothing compared with the great glory that will be shown in us. Our problems are *"momentary";* they are temporary. They won't last.

I may be in the valley now, but I'm coming out. I may be financially strapped now, but I'm going to do better. I may be emotionally drained, but I'm going to bounce back. I may not see a way out of this mess at the moment, but God is able. If I can just hold my peace and let the Lord fight my battle, if I can just hold out until tomorrow, if I can just keep the faith through the night, if I just wait on the Lord, God will renew my strength. This trial is temporary. Things will change.

**You have to get ready before you can venture out.**

Life is seasonal. Sometimes it's summer, and things get hot. Sometimes it's fall, and your harvest comes in. Sometimes it's winter, and you are forced inside. There's no movement, no fruit, just stillness. Life is seasonal. No matter what you're going through, it won't always be that way.

Annie Johnson Flint wrote:

> God hath not promised skies always blue,
> Flower-strewn pathways all our lives through;
> God hath not promised sun without rain,
> Joy without sorrow, peace without pain.
>
> But God hath promised strength for the day,
> Rest for the labor, light for the way,
> Grace for the trials, help from above,
> Unfailing sympathy, undying love.

The rain will fall; storms will come. Burdens will press upon you. You will get weary. The valley will get dark, but remember, it's temporary—this will pass. Smile in your storm; it will deepen your appreciation for clear skies. Smile in your pain; it's paving the way for your power. Smile in your struggle; the process is making you strong.

Consider this illustration from nature. It's not easy to become an Emperor butterfly. To emerge into the world, it has to force its way through the neck of a flask-shaped cocoon. Getting through this opening takes hours of intense struggle. The insect must squirm and wiggle and push its way through the confining threads, but without the struggle, it would never be able to fly. It would have to crawl its entire life. It is the pressure on the insect's body that forces essential chemicals into the wings that get it ready for flight. Remember that suffering is temporary.

## Suffering Is Preparatory

Romans 8:19–21 says, *"For all creation is waiting eagerly for that future day when God will reveal who his children really are. Against its will, everything on earth was subjected to God's curse. All creation anticipates the day…"* (NLT). What day is being anticipated? What is our hope? *"All creation anticipates the day when it will join God's children in glorious freedom from death and decay"* (v. 21 NLT). What we go through is preparatory. Isn't that exciting news? God has a purpose, even for our difficulties.

God has a plan, and that is our hope. God is working things out and preparing us for what He has for us. We cannot see it. We cannot touch it. We can perceive it only in our hearts by faith. God has not given up on creation. He has not stepped away from the world: that's our hope.

God is working in and through the children of God to restore the world, reclaim the world, reunite the world, and redeem the world. That's the goal. That's the hope we have in our suffering. As you go through what you're going through, you are being prepared. God is getting you ready for a higher level of blessing.

God wants to use you in a greater way. In order to make you, first He's going to break you. The suffering will purify you, clarify your motives, rectify your behaviors, and nullify your excuses. Your suffering is preparatory. Jesus said, *"Let not your heart be troubled; you believe in God, believe also in Me"* (John 14:1). It's not what happens *to* you, but what happens *in* you that really matters. The truth is something that we can put our hope in. Suffering is passing and preparatory.

## Suffering Is Painful

I realize that this point might seem obvious, but let me elaborate. The first thing that pain tells you is that you are alive. As long as you are alive, there is always the possibility that things can change. That is a source of hope. You're hurting, but you're still here. Suffering didn't take you out. It didn't kill you. It's rough, but somehow you're holding on. You must be stronger than you thought you were. You can take more than you thought you could. You're still alive. Isn't that a blessing?

Other people came *to*, but didn't come *through*. But you're still here! The enemy took his best shot, and you survived. You're hurting, but you're here; bruised, but blessed; aching, but alive. Romans 8:22–24 says,

> *For we know that the whole creation groans and labors with birth pangs together until now. Not only that, but we also who have the firstfruits of the Spirit, even we ourselves groan within ourselves, eagerly waiting for the adoption, the redemption of our body. For we were saved in this hope.*

There's hope in this pain. It's going somewhere. Expect something. Like a woman in labor, you are groaning while you're bearing fruit. Your suffering is painful, but it's a process. There's a product at the conclusion of your pain. That's God's promise. God is working in you to produce something. You are being changed. You are being transformed. It does not yet appear what you are going to be, but you know that when the labor is over, there will be joy.

First Corinthians 15:42–44 says, *"The body is sown in corruption, it is raised in incorruption. It is sown in dishonor, it is raised in glory. It is sown in weakness, it is raised in power. It is sown a natural body, it is raised a spiritual body."* It is begun in time, but finished in eternity. You can deal with this temporary pain because you know now that you are an eternal project.

One day your imperfection will give way to perfection. Your old body will be traded in for a new one. You'll trade your pain for power, your aches for assurance, your mess for a miracle, your burden for a blessing, your cross for a crown. Revelation 21:3–4 in the *New International Version* says,

> *Now the dwelling of God is with men, and he will live with them. They will be his people, and God himself will be with them and be their God. He will wipe every tear from their eyes. There will be no more death or mourning or crying or pain, for the old order of things has passed away.*

There will be no more suffering, heartache, or hurt feelings. That's our hope. That's something we can look forward to when we're in pain. Knowing what God has promised for His children is a source of hope.

## God Will Provide

God provides for us in our suffering. Romans 8:26 says, *"The Spirit also helps in our weaknesses. For we do not know what we should pray for as we ought, but the Spirit Himself makes intercession for us with groanings which cannot be uttered."* That verse gives us hope. When we're suffering, the Holy Spirit prays for us.

Have you ever been in a situation that was so complex, so heavy, and so hard that you didn't know what to pray for or even how to pray? Here's some hope. God understands what we're going through, and even when we can't verbalize it—when we can't put it into words—He looks past our words and interprets our hearts.

Jesus can identify with our pain because He *"was in all points tempted as we are"* (Heb. 4:15). Jesus knows what you're going through. So when you're suffering, don't worry about praying special words or phrases; just talk to God. Be real with Him. Be honest with God.

Say, "Lord, I'm hurting. I don't understand why I'm going through what I'm going through, but I believe it's passing. I believe it's preparatory. I acknowledge it's painful, but You promised to provide for me. You promised to help me. You promised to be with me." I am a witness that God will step in on time. God will help you, walk with you, comfort you, and lift you up. Even though you can't see God, He will be right there by your side.

A youth group was enjoying a week of climbing and cave exploration near Fredericksburg, Texas. David Yankton, an experienced wilderness guide, was leading them. He brought along his six-year-old daughter, Kelly. On the second day, David led the group into a cave and allowed only one flashlight.

At the entrance, the group moved rapidly, but as they walked deeper and deeper into the cave, the darkness thickened. Finally, the cave became so dark that they couldn't take a step without clear directions from the person in front of them. At one point in the darkness, Kelly panicked and screamed, "Daddy, don't leave me." And from the darkness came her father's voice, saying, "I'm right here in front of you. Don't be afraid."

Sound familiar? When we're suffering or struggling, we're not in it alone. God is in front of us, around us, behind us, and within us to help us.

## Suffering Is Profitable

God has a purpose in our problems. The Bible tells us, *"And we know that all things work together for good to those who love God, to those who are the called according to His purpose"* (Rom. 8:28). Paul didn't say all things are good. There are many bad things in the world. God's will is not always done. That's why we are to pray for it to be done.

Yet the Scripture says that God takes even our mistakes, errors, problems, and desperate circumstances and uses them together for good. God puts them together like a jigsaw puzzle and brings a positive purpose and profitable product out of them. Shakespeare said, "Sweet are the uses of adversity."[4] Know that, in your suffering, God is working for you.

Dr. Gardner C. Taylor, Pastor Emeritus of Concord Baptist Church in New York and a prince of preachers, once told a young preacher who was complaining about the trial that he was called on to endure, "Young man, while you're going through the struggle, let it bless you. Let it make your faith deeper. Let your conscience become clearer. Let your hope become stronger. Let your commitment grow more resolute."

"While you're going through the struggle, let it bless you." There are notes in you that you cannot sing until you suffer, visions you cannot see until you bear the cross, joys you cannot know until your pain is deep and your burden is heavy. Let your struggle bless you. As one songwriter wrote,

Be not dismayed whate'er be-tide;
God will take care of you.
Beneath His wings of love abide;
God will take care of you.

All you may need He will provide;
God will take care of you.
Nothing you ask will be denied;
God will take care of you.

God will take care of you,
Through ev'ry day, o'er all the way.
He will take care of you;
God will take care of you.[5]

The bottom line of Romans 8:28 is that God has a purpose behind your suffering. When you have a problem, realize that the way you're looking at the problem can be the problem. Look beyond the problem and remember five things: it's passing, preparatory, painful, provisional, and profitable. God is working in it, through it, and even in spite of it for your good. You must choose your perspective. Suffering *will* come. You will either hope or mope, grumble or be grateful; the choice is up to you!

I hope you're not going through major suffering right now and that you can file this lesson away for another time. However, if you are going through a difficult period, or you have a persistent problem to which there seems to be no solution, know that God sees what you're going through. Why not pray this prayer?

## Prayer:

Lord, help me to realize that You see and You care when I hurt. When I groan, You hear me. Lord, I believe You have the power to change my situation, and I ask You to change it. But in the meantime, change me. Make me different. Use my suffering for a positive purpose in my life. Help me to grow through this pain. In Jesus' name, I pray. Amen.

# 14

# MAKE YOUR MOVE

I hesitated and felt like procrastinating, but I knew if I was going to climb the mountain, I had to make a move and climb it one hop at a time." Those were the words spoken by a one-legged amputee after he climbed 14,000 feet to the top of a mountain. There was no magic involved in his reaching his goal. He just had to "make a move."

If you are going to succeed in life, see your dreams realized, and achieve your goals, you have to make a move. Stop talking and begin acting. Stop intending to do, and do. Make your move. The mountain of our hopes, dreams, aspirations, and ambitions beckons us right now. The summit of success, satisfaction, and joy calls to us right now, but we will never reach the peak or scale that lofty height if we don't make a move.

Aiming is fine, but at some point you have to act. Good intentions are wonderful, but intention has to be translated into invention. The challenge for you as you read this chapter is to summon the courage to make your move. What is it right now that you have put off doing that you know you should do? What decision, action, or step do you need to make, but you have found yourself hesitating to do? What are those things about which you keep promising yourself to take action?

> **Planning is good, but at some point, you have to produce.**

What do you keep postponing and making excuses about? Do you find yourself saying things like, "One day, when this happens…"; "As soon as circumstances change…"; "If my ship comes in…"; "If my number comes up…"; "When I get a chance," and so on? If we're going to achieve our goals, realize our dreams, execute our plans, and seize the day, we have to make a move.

Dr. Benjamin E. Mays, former president of Atlanta's Morehouse College, has said,

> It's 11:59 on the clock of destiny, and you've only got a minute, sixty seconds in it, forced upon you, can't refuse it, didn't seek it, didn't choose it, but it's up to you to use it, give account if you abuse it. It's only a minute, but eternity is in it.[1]

Make your move. What is it that keeps us procrastinating and hesitating—caught in the clenches of "shoulda, woulda, coulda"? I believe there are at least five reasons we procrastinate, hesitate, and find it difficult to make our move. Ready for this?

# Reason #1: Doubt

Make no mistake; in all authentic faith, there will be some honest doubt. In fact, the highway to a strong faith runs through the valley of doubt. Doubt is an integral part of making important commitments, but when your doubt begins to overwhelm your faith, you're in trouble. Doubt is the growing edge of faith, but when your doubts become your entire focus, you have a problem. Doubt can paralyze your progress, stifle your success, drown your enthusiasm, and suffocate your growth. Doubt is the first reason that we hesitate and procrastinate.

# Reason #2: Discouragement

After the crucifixion of Jesus, the Bible reports that the disciples went home and shut their doors in fear. (See John 20:19.) Peter went back to his boat and said, *"I am going fishing"* (John 21:3). They were deeply discouraged. We might as well be honest: everybody gets discouraged sometimes. Discouragement is universal, reoccurring, and highly contagious. If we hang around people who are discouraged, it's only a matter of time before we'll be infected. Discouragement can still our feet, stop our hands, and delay our plans. Sometimes we don't move out and move on because we're just plain discouraged.

# Reason #3: Depression

When we feel powerless, as if there's nothing we can do, we get depressed. When we're emotionally or physically exhausted, we are prime candidates for depression. Things will seem bleaker than they are, problems will seem stronger than they are, burdens will seem heavier than they are—*not because they are,* but because depression has sapped our strength. Doubt, discouragement, and depression cause us to procrastinate.

# Reason #4: Despair

Have you ever felt like giving up? Our world is filled with people who have given up on their dreams, surrendered their ambitions, and thrown away their hopes. Doors of opportunity have been closed before them, opportunities for betterment and blessing have been restricted, options have been aborted, and the possibility of enablement has been truncated. As a result, they gave up.

After Judas betrayed Jesus, when the weight of guilt pressed heavily on his conscience, he just gave up. He went out and committed suicide. When you feel as though there's no reason to go on, when you feel as if life is hopeless, hesitation and procrastination will hold you handcuffed to your present situation.

# Reason #5: Defeat

Sometimes our best-laid plans fall apart. Projects collapse, deals fall through, orders are cancelled, and marriages don't work. Everybody experiences defeat.

**Big shots are just little shots that keep on shooting.**

Henry Ward Beecher said, "Defeat is a school in which truth always grows strong." When we suffer defeat, it's easy to give up trying. The movement had been promising, the miracles had been plenteous, the Master had walked in power, but now He had been crucified. The disciples had seen it. They had witnessed it with their own eyes. Now He was dead. And that was enough to take the wind out of their sails. Peter was drowning in regret.

On the night he denied Jesus, Peter learned some things about himself. In that deep hurt of self-realization, he discovered that he was not as strong as he thought he was. One writer said, "That which hurts, instructs." Peter learned some things about himself: too much talking, not enough trusting; too much conversation, not enough character; too much external show, not enough internal development. On the weekend of the Resurrection, doubt, discouragement, depression, despair, and defeat had free reign. Everybody was infected—everyone except Mary Magdalene.

She had watched from a distance when they crucified Jesus on Friday. She had gone home in tears when they took Him down from the cross. Mary Magdalene had been redeemed from a painful past. She faced the peril of the present moment by getting up and going to the tomb, even though she knew that it was heavily guarded.

She summoned the courage to make her move. In doing so, she learned a dynamic lesson from which you and I can learn: when you make a move in faith, when you step out in the strength of the Lord, when you acknowledge God and put your love for Him first, you will discover these five great truths.

## Your Fears Are Wrong

Mary and the other women had come to the tomb afraid. On Friday, their dreams had died, and their hopes had been crucified.

They knew Joseph of Arimethea had taken charge of Jesus' body and had wrapped it in a linen shroud. Joseph had laid Christ in a brand-new, rock-hewn family tomb.

The women knew that Pilate was fearful that somebody would steal Jesus' body and then erroneously report that He had risen from the dead. Pilate had dispatched a military watch of Roman soldiers to make the tomb secure by putting a seal over the stone and guarding the tomb, keeping out necromancers, prowlers, and wild animals.

The stone was there, but the women couldn't move it. The guards were there, but they couldn't fight them. The seal was tight, but they couldn't break it. The women were afraid, but when they arrived at the tomb, they discovered their fears were wrong. An angel told the women, *"Do not be afraid, for I know that you seek Jesus who was crucified. He is not here; for He is risen, as He said"* (Matt. 28:5–6).

Likewise, so many of the fears, phobias, anxieties, and worries that keep us paralyzed and immobilized have no basis in reality at all. When the women went to the tomb that morning, they discovered that their fears were wrong. They were not expecting Jesus to be alive. In fact, this news of His resurrection was a great surprise.

Mark 16:8 says, *"Trembling and bewildered, the women went out and fled from the tomb. They said nothing to anyone, because they were afraid"* (NIV). Cruel executions don't usually become joyful resurrections. Sealing tombs is customary, but opening tombs is uncommon. We are accustomed to putting people *in* the grave, not accustomed to their *coming out.* But Scripture says, *"Suddenly there was a great earthquake; for an angel of the Lord came down from heaven and rolled aside the stone and sat on it"* (Matt. 28:2 TLB).

The angel came down so that we could rise up. He sat down so that we might stand up. He sat on the stone as an indication that no obstacle can stop, impede, or hinder the dynamic purpose of God for our lives. He sat down to indicate that God was creating a whole new paradigm, producing an entirely new possibility, bringing something to be that we had never seen before. Your fears are wrong.

## Your God Is Able

The angel said, *"He is not here; for He is risen, as He said"* (Matt. 28:6). Something had happened. An earthquake had toppled the foundations of hell, shaken loose the gates of death, and moved the stone away from the tomb. This was no ordinary earthquake. It could not be measured on the Richter scale.

**Shaking is a part of God's making.** The word for *earthquake* in the Greek is *seismos*, and it is defined as "a cosmic shaking, a rearrangement in the order of things, a change in the modus operandi." God has shaken us loose from the narrow restrictions of race, the constricted corridors of gender, and the cruel confines of economic privilege. Before God can make, God first has to shake. When God permits life to shake you, it's because He is getting ready to make you.

God raised Christ up, and, likewise, God has raised us so that we can live again, dream again, hope again, and try again. Praise the name of the Lord! Some people have no awareness of the power of God. They have no consciousness of the hope, joy, and victory of the Resurrection; but what is objectively true and substantially real does not require a human mind to be aware of it, a human heart to love it, a human eye to see it, or a single human heart to appreciate it.

Birds are singing today, even if we can't hear them. Lilies are blooming today, even if we don't see them. Christ is risen now to bring to the whole creation a new dimension of life, hope, power, and joy, even if some people don't acknowledge it.

Aren't you glad that you're not spiritually unconscious, morally dysfunctional, or religiously disabled? Aren't you glad that you aren't lying somewhere in a coma of faithlessness unaware of the goodness, grace, and glory of almighty God? Aren't you glad that you can testify for yourself that something has happened? Aren't you glad that God is able?

Today is the day for you, like Mary, to step past your fears and make your move. The angel said, *"He is not here; for He is risen, as He said"* (Matt. 28:6). The power of the resurrection is available to us. Don't tell me you can't make it; God is able. Don't tell me you don't have resources, strength, or time; God is able. Whatever you need, God has it. Whatever you want, God can supply it.

## Your Access Is Assured

The angel went on to tell the women, *"Come, see the place where the Lord lay. And go quickly and tell His disciples that He is risen from the dead, and indeed He is going before you into Galilee; there you will see Him. Behold, I have told you"* (Matt. 28:6–7). The angel spoke to Mary Magdalene—a woman (that's first)—whose past was filled with pain (that's second). Both of those details should have been reasons to block her progress. She was a female in a male dominated culture. Her résumé was less than impressive. She had no pedigree, social standing, position, network, or connections; yet she was invited in. This is a new revelation for a new situation. The message behind the angel's words said, "You can come in, Mary. I know in the past, they've kept you out. You have been defined by your actions, limited by your gender, and confined by your condition, but that's over now because Christ is risen!"

God is saying to you today, "Come in. I have something I want you to see." We've all experienced being locked out, kept out, and blocked out. We've stood face-to-face with some impregnable barrier. Yet, thanks be to God, the foundations have been shaken, the tomb is open, the way is clear, and our access is assured—all because Jesus Christ, Calvary's conquering Hero, has ended our nightmares, liberated our potential, broken the stranglehold of our addictions, moved the barricade of our fear, shaken loose our destructive impulses, and made a way out of no way!

Today we celebrate the grace of God that has given us access to the blessing, joy, and power of God. We can know God, love Him, and talk and walk with Him. We have access, and when God opens a door, nobody can shut it. When God makes a way, no one can block it. Motivated by the mercy that met her, Mary ran from the tomb to tell the good news. That brings us to the final movement of this magnificent story.

## When You Move, Your Miracle Will Meet You

Not *before* you move, but *as* you move, your miracle will meet you. The Bible says,

> So they went out quickly from the tomb with fear and great joy, and ran to bring His disciples word. And as they went to tell His disciples, behold, Jesus met them, saying, "Rejoice!" So they came and held Him by the feet and worshiped Him.
>
> (Matt. 28:8–9)

They were rejoicing in the privilege of participation. Joyous yet terrified over what had happened, they were running to take the news to the disciples. As they were on their way, Jesus met them. It's *as we move* that God will bless us, that a miracle will meet us. So often we sit or stand with our hands idle, our feet still, and our minds blank as we wait for something to happen. But something has already happened, and, if you believe, it's time to get moving.

**Nothing will move until you do.**

Nothing will change until you do. Often, it's not that we're waiting on God; most of time, God is waiting on us. God is waiting on us to start the business, develop the plan, search for resources, create the connection, and stretch out in faith. The message of this passage is that *as you move, a miracle will meet you on the way.* Jesus met them. They came face-to-face with the One whom they didn't expect.

## Your Failure Isn't Final

*"Then Jesus said to them, 'Do not be afraid. Go and tell My brethren to go to Galilee, and there they will see Me'"* (Matt. 28:10). Don't close

the book of your life. Don't draw premature conclusions. Just because you fell down doesn't mean you have to stay down. Tell the devil he's a liar and a deceiver, too. God's not through blessing you. I know you've made mistakes, fallen short, and made some wrong turns, but that's your past; it doesn't have to be your future.

There is still time, life, energy, hope, and power to make your move. Your life is not done. Your dreams are not illusions. Your hopes are not in vain. Your aspirations are still within the realm of possibility. Defeat is never terminal unless you accept it. Make your move.

> **Defeat is never terminal unless you accept it.**

### Prayer:

> Dear Lord, sometimes I am paralyzed by my fears and doubts. I question whether You could really be calling *me* to do something for *You*. I ask You to forgive me for my hesitation and procrastination. Free me from the baggage of past failures and nagging self-doubts. With gratitude, I realize that You can use even my failures and weaknesses for Your glory. Help me to walk in confidence and faith, knowing that You will guide my course. With renewed faith, I step into my future, excited to see what You are going to do in and through me. In Jesus' name, I pray. Amen.

# 15

# DON'T GIVE UP

O n one occasion, Jesus told a parable that is a study in con-
trasts. The characters who make up this drama are a powerful judge and a powerless widow. Jesus began by giving us a
description of the judge: *"There was in a certain city a judge who did
not fear God nor regard man"* (Luke 18:2). This judge was hard-
boiled, unsympathetic, and calloused. He didn't give a hoot about
people; he was a real rascal.

Then Jesus continued, *"There was a widow in that city; and she came
to him, saying, 'Get justice for me from my adversary'"* (v. 3). We don't
know who she was or what her problem was, but we do know that
she was in distress, and she was persistent.

The word *"widow"* in the verse means literally "left empty and
forsaken." It indicates that in that time and culture, widows had
absolutely no rights at all. They were alone, forsaken, often neglected, and at the bottom of the social ladder. Without help from
their families, widows had little or no resources and meager support outside of alms, offerings, and donations from charitable citi-
zens.

She was in distress, but she was no pushover. She had a problem,
and she took it to this stonyhearted judge. He refused to give in to
her or give her what she wanted. He unwittingly entered into a

battle of wills. *"For some time he refused. But finally he said to himself,*
*'Even though I don't fear God or care about men, yet because this widow*
*keeps bothering me, I will see that she gets justice'"* (Luke 18:4–5 NIV).

One can imagine that the disciples were laughing by now at the
thought of this small, powerless widow intimidating this prestig-
ious, powerful judge. She probably said, "Your Honor, this isn't
fair." There are many things in life that just don't seem fair. God
never said that life would be fair. You have to get over it and
press on.

This woman had no resources, but persistence; no tools, but persistence; no weapons, but persistence. She kept going back. She
became a badgering nuisance. Finally, acknowledging that he had
met his match, the judge gave in.

He said, *"Because this widow keeps bothering me, I will see that she gets*
*justice, so that she won't eventually wear me out with her coming!'"* (v. 5
NIV). In the Greek, the phrase *"wear me out"* literally means, "to
give a black eye or a bruise." The judge might have thought, "I'm
afraid this lady is going to hit me. She is so aggressive that she
might whack me upside my head. She keeps asking and asking.
She's getting on my nerves. I want some peace and quiet. I'm just
going to give her what she wants."

Is this how we are to respond to God—just wear Him out and
wear Him down, just keep fussing and complaining until He finally gets tired and says, "Just to shut your mouth, just to get you
off My back, I'm going to give you what you want"? Is that what
God is saying to you and me? Is that what this passage is teaching? Not at all.

The point of the passage is this: if a heartless judge will respond
to a need, how much more can we count on God who loves us to
help us out? Verses 7–8 say, *"And shall God not avenge His own elect*
*who cry out day and night to Him, though He bears long with them? I*
*tell you that He will avenge them speedily."* The point of the story is
that God is eager to answer our prayers.

We don't have to beg, gripe, complain, or pester God. God is not like the judge in these verses. He is eager to answer our prayers. And that brings us to these questions: Why, then, do we need to be persistent? How come our answers don't come immediately? Why should we keep on praying when the answer doesn't arrive in our timetable? I want to give you four reasons to keep on praying when there's no answer.

## Persistent Praying Helps Us to Focus on God

The purpose of persistent prayer is not to remind God, but to remind us where our blessings come from and who is really in charge of the world. God is our Source. He does not suffer from amnesia. He never forgets a promise. When we pray God's promise, when we believe His promise, when we claim His promise, we focus on what God can and will do for us.

God wants us to remember that He alone is the Source of our blessings. He alone answers prayer. He alone can make a way out of no way. The apostle Paul says, *"And my God shall supply all your need according to His riches in glory by Christ Jesus"* (Phil. 4:19). God wants us to see Him as the Source of our blessings, the Reason for our hope, the Point of our praise, and the Dispenser of our deliverance.

We are to look to God. Persistent prayer requires looking not at your circumstances, deficiencies, disappointments, or distractions, but at God. Persistent prayer focuses our attention on God. One very popular television minister taught that people who ask God for something and then ask again don't have faith. While I have great respect for him, I prefer the perspective of Jesus because, while this man is a child of God, Jesus emerged from the bosom of God. And Jesus taught that we *"should always pray and not give up"* (Luke 18:1 NIV).

**Persistent prayer does not reveal a lack of faith.**

In fact, when we really consider it, it takes more faith to pray and not receive an immediate answer and yet continue to pray than it does to pray one time and wait to see what happens. Persistent prayer isn't blackmailing, cajoling, or manipulating God into answering us.

Have you noticed how easy it is for us to look everywhere and to everybody and to everything to solve our problems, rectify our dilemmas, and fix our situations instead of looking to God? We turn to our friends, our families, counselors, the government, luck, the lotto, rabbit's feet, horoscopes, psychic hotlines, and lovelines—to everything and anybody except the Lord.

But Psalm 105:4 instructs us, *"Seek the LORD and His strength; seek His face evermore!"* The songwriter raised these questions,

> Where do I hide till the storms have all passed over?
> Where do I run to when the winds of sorrow threaten?
> Is there a refuge in the time of tribulation?[1]

And she provided the answer: "When-a my soul needs consolation, I go to the Rock." Persistent praying focuses us on God. And often God will delay our answers in order to teach us to focus on Him.

## Persistent Praying Filters Our Requests

Every day when I make coffee, I first put a filter in the pot. Although I put coffee grounds in the holder, I don't want coffee grounds to come out. I want just the coffee, not the grounds; and the filter separates them from the coffee. Likewise, time is a filter for our prayers; it separates whims from deep desires. A delayed answer to our prayers gives us time to clarify what it is we really want. Many times, we don't want what we think we want. Many of our prayers are too vague to be serviceable and too general to be functional. We pray, "God, give me some 'things.'" What "things" did you have in mind? How will you know when you have received them? We ask, "God, bless my life." Sometimes a blessing comes wrapped up inside a burden. Is this what you mean: "Lord, give me more burdens"?

Persistent praying and waiting give us time to clarify our requests and to become more specific. Don't be general. Don't be vague. "Lord, help me with my kids." No. "Lord, give me the wisdom day by day to nurture and rear these children so that they will become spiritual, responsible, loving, independent adults."

Be specific. Don't pray, "Lord, give me a spouse." Instead, pray, "Lord, by Your grace, give me a positive partner with whom I can share a growing, mutually beneficial relationship that will blossom by Your grace into a progressive, spiritually centered, financially grounded, socially conscious, radiantly happy, absolutely exclusive, melodiously monogamous experience of joy." Be specific, and then wait. Waiting helps us to refine and purify our requests. It helps us to get beyond what we think we want to what we really need.

**Waiting gives us time to clarify what we want.**

A story is told of two men traveling aboard a boat that was shipwrecked during a terrible storm at sea. Once they washed up on a deserted island, they both agreed that they should turn to God. One day, in delirium and disagreement, they began to argue about who had the most profound prayers, whom God was inclined to listen to. This argument drove them apart.

They each took to separate parts of the island and continued their prayers. The first man prayed for food. The next morning when he woke up, he discovered a fruit-bearing tree five feet from where he was. The other man's parcel of land remained barren. After a week, the first man felt lonely, so he prayed for a wife. That night, another ship wrecked on the reefs. The only survivor was a woman. The other man remained on his side of the island alone. The first man prayed for a house, clothes, and more food. All of his requests were answered, while the other man had received nothing.

Finally, the first man prayed for a boat, so that he and his wife could leave the island. In the morning, they discovered a boat docked on their side of the island. They got on the boat and decided to leave the other man on the island. The first man thought to himself, "Something must be wrong with that guy's prayer life; he must not have the anointing. Not one of his prayers has been answered."

As the couple were about to leave, they both heard a voice booming from heaven. It asked, "Why are you leaving your companion?"

The man answered, "Lord, my blessings are mine alone. I prayed for them, and You gave them to me. What You have given me is for me. You didn't answer any of his prayers, so I knew he wasn't praying right."

God said, "You are so mistaken. He had only one prayer, and I answered it. If it were not for his prayer, you would never have received any of the things you have."

The first man said, "Tell me, what did he pray for? Why do I owe him anything?" God said, "He had one prayer. He asked me to answer all of your prayers, and I did."

Persistent prayer filters our requests; it purifies our prayers. It reminds us that we didn't get where we are on our own. People prayed for me. They had me on their minds. They took the time and prayed for me, and I'm so glad they did. What about you? Delayed prayers give us space to ask ourselves, "Do I really want it? How bad do I want it?" If I don't want it bad enough to keep praying for it, I don't want it bad enough.

Zechariah 13:9 says, *"I will...test them as gold is tested. They will call on My name, and I will answer them."* Time separates deep longings from mere whims. I can testify today that I've prayed for things and sometimes decided during the delay that I didn't really want them after all. They weren't what I needed. A delay is not a denial: it's just a test.

All of us are a lot like tea bags: you don't know what's really inside us until you put us in hot water and keep us there. God delays the answer in order to test us. It's not that God doesn't want to give it to us; God wants us to clarify if we really want it. Do you want it enough to keep praying? Do you want it enough to hold on when it doesn't make sense to do so anymore?

Do you want it enough to endure criticism, walk through ridicule, risk abandonment, and grapple with loneliness and misunderstanding in pursuit of that dream? How bad do you want it? Many times during a delay, you will find that you modify and change your prayer; you clarify it until it becomes crystal clear. Jeremiah 29:13 says, *"You will seek Me and find Me, when you search for Me with all your heart."*

Nothing worthwhile is accomplished with halfhearted prayers. "O God, please give 'this' to me...maybe." Halfhearted prayers. God says, *"Search for Me with all your heart."* Do you really want it? Persistent prayer helps us to focus on God. It helps us to filter our requests.

## Persistent Praying Prepares Us for the Answer

Our prayers are usually smaller than God's desire for us. Surprise! You're praying for something, but God wants to do something bigger. He wants to do something greater. He wants to do more. Ephesians 3:20 says, *"Now glory be to God! By his mighty power at work within us, he is able to accomplish infinitely more than we would ever dare to ask or hope"* (NLT).

God wants to do more in us, with us, and through us. Sometimes we ask for a small blessing, and God denies it. Why? Because He wants to give us a bigger one. God wants to do something greater, and He uses time to get us ready for it. I'm thankful that some of my prayers have not been answered in my time schedule, because I wouldn't have been ready for them at that particular time. God had to prepare me.

There are changes God wants to make in me. People say, "Prayer changes things." That's true, but prayer also changes us. Prayer will change you. God is more interested in you than He is in things. He is more interested in developing your character than altering your circumstances. God wants to make some changes in our lives, and that's often why our answers are delayed.

The greater the work that God wants to do in you, the longer it will take. When God wants to make a mushroom, it takes six hours. When He wants to make an oak tree, it takes sixty years. What do you want to be: a mushroom or an oak tree? During what appears to be a delay, God is preparing us. Many times, just as soon as we change, the answer comes.

Again, often it's not that we're waiting on God; He is waiting on us. When we're ready, the windows of heaven open, the answer comes, the healing is granted, and the river of blessing flows. Prayer is not a tug-of-war with God, where we're trying to convince Him to see our point of view. Our struggles are primarily with ourselves.

I read about a missionary who prayed for eight years that one person would be saved in the area where he was serving. No one was converted for eight years, yet he kept on praying. Finally, he began to pray, "Lord, do what You want to do through me in this place."

The next morning, the whole tribe of twelve thousand people showed up at his house, having made the decision to be baptized. He hadn't been ready for the blessing. God had to prepare him. God had to prepare them. And in God's own time, He answered in a bigger, greater, and grander way than the missionary could ever have imagined. God's delays help us to focus on Him. They filter our requests and prepare us for the answer.

## Persistent Praying Strengthens Our Faith

Prayer and faith go hand in hand. Faith is like a muscle; it grows by being stretched. You've never been stretched until you have to wait. Praying persistently is a faith-building exercise. Waiting tests your faith. A mark of immaturity is the inability to wait. Galatians 6:9 says, *"Let us not grow weary while doing good, for in due season we shall reap if we do not lose heart."* God is saying to us, "Be patient. Hang in there. Hold on. The harvest is coming. Don't give up. Instead, look up."

I read a story about a man who was called to be a missionary to Africa. He believed that God had called him to go there to share the Gospel and to work among people mired in poverty and despair. He kept waiting and waiting for God to bless him with the money to afford the tickets to go to Africa. One night, while he was praying about it, the Spirit of God spoke to him and raised this question: "What would you do if you already had the money for the tickets?"

He said, "I'd go and get on the plane!" Then the Spirit of the Lord spoke to him again and asked, "Do you believe that I am your Provider? Am I the Source of all your needs?" "Yes," he answered. "Then, pack your things and go to the airport."

He told his wife what had happened, and what he believed. They announced to their church the next Sunday that they would be leaving. They were on their way to Africa, knowing that they had only enough money to get about fifty miles down the road. But the church gave them a big farewell party. They bought the tickets for the train, went fifty miles down the road, and that was it.

They sat in the train station, saying to themselves, "Don't we look foolish? God said, 'Step out in faith,' and we did it, and nothing is happening. Here we are fifty miles away from home. What are we going to do now?"

God spoke to the man and asked, "If you had the money, what would you do?" He said, "I'd buy a ticket." God told him, "Get in line."

There was a line of eighteen people, but the man got in line. He stood there, and the line kept getting smaller and smaller. He had no money, and he kept thinking, "I am going to look really stupid when I get to the counter and don't have any money."

Finally, there were just two people ahead of him. Before he knew it, he said out loud, "Lord, I look stupid here!" Suddenly the man right in front of him turned around and said, "I've changed my mind. I'm not going to go. Here! You can have my money." And he took off. The man and his wife bought the tickets and went to Africa.

God's timing was perfect. God's delays are not denials. Delays help us to focus on God. They clarify our vision and prepare us for greater blessings. The longer you have to wait, the greater your miracle may be. Delays strengthen, test, challenge, and develop our faith. Jesus concluded the parable of the persistent widow by saying, *"I tell you that He will avenge them speedily. Nevertheless, when the Son of Man comes, will He really find faith on the earth?"* (Luke 18:8). Faith and prayer go together. That's what we have to remember. We must pray, but we must also have faith.

The size of your prayers is determined by your perception of God. How large is your perception of Him? If you look at your prayer life, you can tell. What are you praying for? Something tiny? Something you can do yourself? If God is your Partner, your plans should be larger. Faith and prayer go together. Anytime your prayers are delayed, two things are going on: God is testing your faith, and satan is contesting it.

## Your persistence demonstrates your faith.

Jesus admired this widow because she refused to give up. She was persistent, tenacious, and determined. How quickly do you give up when the answer is not immediate? Do you lose heart? Do you want to quit? Faith persists.

How do you pray persistently? In Luke 11, Jesus told another parable with the same point: don't give up; look up. (See verses 5–9.) Jesus said, *"Ask, and it will be given to you; seek, and you will find;*

*knock, and it will be opened to you. For everyone who asks receives, and he who seeks finds, and to him who knocks it will be opened"* (Luke 11:9–10). Keep on asking. Keep on knocking. Keep on seeking. What we often do is go up to the door, knock, and run away before it opens. How many people would you talk to on the phone if you let it ring only once? Keep on seeking. Keep on knocking— not to convince God or to wear Him out, but for your benefit.

Daniel Boone was a famous settler in the Kentucky area. He traveled all over the wilderness. One day somebody asked him, "Have you ever been lost?" Boone answered, "No, I've never been lost. I've been bewildered sometimes for days and sometimes for up to a week. But I just keep on going." Have you ever felt that way? You're bewildered, and you don't know what's going on. But you just keep on going.

Maybe your relationship with someone is in trouble. You've been praying for months, and you're ready to throw in the towel, but you just keep on going. Maybe you can't find the right job. You're facing a serious illness. You're stuck at home with diapers all over the house. You feel like the widow in the parable—powerless, hopeless, and helpless. Here's the point of that story: don't give up. Hang in there. Hold on. Don't quit.

Look up. Don't despair. Turn to prayer. Don't cave in to discouragement. Persistence will win the crown. Expect a miracle. It's worth another try. That's what God says to us.

*"Always pray"* (Luke 18:1 NIV), and never give up. What is it that causes you to want to give up today? What do you want to give up on? Do you want to give up on your marriage? Your children? Your job? Yourself? Your parents? Your dream? Don't give up; look up.

It may be that some of you have never opened your life up to Jesus Christ. I don't know how you can make it without His supernatural power. You were never meant to live on your own strength. I invite you today to open your heart to Christ—to a new relationship, not a religion. You may be Protestant, Catholic, Jewish, Buddhist, or Mormon. But here's what really matters: Do you have a personal, authentic relationship with God?

## Prayer:

Gracious God, thank You for those who are opening their hearts to You right now for the very first time. Enable them to find a church that will help them to grow in their faith. Thank You for those who came to You discouraged, but who now are soaring on the wings of eagles. Give to all of us the power to keep on, press on, and live on for You—no matter what challenges life brings our way. We give You the little we have and pray that You will maximize it for Your glory. In the name of Jesus, we pray. Amen.

# ABOUT THE AUTHOR

Dr. Lance D. Watson is Senior Pastor of the Saint Paul's Baptist Church of Richmond, Virginia. The church's mission is to effectively reach and teach 7,000 persons by the year 2005 and nurture them in 700 small groups to realize their maximum potential. Its vision is to touch the world with love—by communicating the positive power of faith, by identifying needs and meeting them, by recognizing problems and solving them, and by finding hurts and healing them. Over the last decade, Saint Paul's has experienced phenomenal growth and serves as spiritual home to more than 6,000 "people on the grow."

Dr. Watson is very active in his community. He has been chosen as an African-American Role Model by Channel 6 and Consolidated Bank, noted as a "Great Communicator" by WWBT Channel 12, and recognized as an "Outstanding Contributor to Education" by the Richmond Public School Board. He serves as host of the widely viewed television program, *Positive Power*, and as Chairman of the Board of Directors for Nia, Inc. of Greater Richmond, a community-based economic development corporation.

Dr. Watson is a three-time *summa cum laude* graduate of Wayne State University in Detroit. He holds undergraduate degrees in Philosophy and Psychology and has a graduate degree in Guidance and Counseling. He also holds a graduate degree from the Presbyterian School of Christian Education at Union Theological Seminary and the Master of Divinity from the Samuel DeWitt Proctor School of Theology at Virginia Union University of Richmond, Virginia. Recently, he received an honorary doctorate from Richmond Virginia Seminary.

For more information on telecasts, conferences, products, and events featuring Lance Watson, contact:

Positive Power
2600 East Marshall Street
Richmond, Virginia 23223-7344
(804) 643-4000
http://www.lancewatson.com

# NOTES

## Chapter 1: Elevate Your Expectation
[1] See A. A. Milne, *Winnie-the-Pooh* (New York: E. P. Dutton, 1926).
[2] See Lionel Tiger, *Optimism: The Biology of Hope* (New York: Simon and Schuster, 1979).

## Chapter 2: Alter Your Attitude
[1] This quote came from the following Web site: www. cybernation.com.
[2] This quote came from the following Web site: www. cybernation.com.

## Chapter 3: Go for the Goal
[1] The speech from which this quotation was taken is available at the following Web site: www.cs.umb.edu/jfklibrary/j052561.htm.
[2] This is a quotation from Socrates.

## Chapter 4: Cultivate Your Confidence
[1] This quote came from the following Web site: www. phnet.fi/ public/mamaa1/frames.htm.
[2] See Victor Goertzel and Mildred George Goertzel, *Cradles of Eminence* (Boston: Little, Brown, 1962). Pay special attention to "Reconnoitering among the Findings" on pages 272–274.
[3] These examples came from "Stories about Persistence in Life" found on the Web site: www.gospelcom.net/cgi/dw/1997/06/04/.

## Chapter 5: Conquer Your Circumstances
[1] From *The Mourning Bride*, Act 3, Scene 8.
[2] Words and Music by Horatio R. Palmer, 1868.
[3] The author heard Dr. Sampson make this statement in a Contemporary Theology Class at Tabernacle Baptist Church in Detroit, Michigan.

## Chapter 6: Proceed with Passion
[1] These lyrics are from the song "What a Friend We Have in Jesus." Words by Joseph M. Scriven, ca. 1855; Music by Charles C. Converse, 1868.

## Chapter 7: Live in Love
[1] Sam Keen, *Fire in the Belly: On Being a Man* (New York: Bantam, 1991).
[2] Robert Bly, *Iron John: A Book about Men* (Reading, MA: Addison-Wesley, 1990).
[3] See Charles Harold Dodd, *The Interpretation of the Fourth Gospel* (Cambridge, UK: 1968).

## Chapter 8: Pursue Your Purpose
[1] Lewis Carroll, *Alice in Wonderland* (New York: W. W. Norton, 1971). See chapter six, "Pig and Pepper," for this conversation between Alice and the Cat.
[2] This quotation appears in the section entitled "Economy" in Henry David Thoreau's *Walden, or Life in the Woods.*

## Chapter 9: Build a Balanced Life
[1] These lyrics are from the song "You Know and I Know" on the album *Different Lifestyles.*
[2] One of the many Internet sites from which you can access this story is http://www.internetoutlet.net/stcvem/stories/crackpot.htm.

## Chapter 10: Confront Your Circumstances
[1] These lyrics are from the song "Amazing Grace," written by John Newton, 1779.

## Chapter 11: Deepen Your Discipline
[1] Attributed to Roy Campanella and available from many Internet sites, including www.uwplatt.edu/~huff/creed.html.

[2] See *Black Diamonds: The Wisdom of Booker T. Washington.* Selected and arranged by Victoria Earle Matthews and edited by Frank Hill. Available from Amazon.com in a reprint edition, 1995.
[3] For further information, go to www.jei.org/Archive/JEIR98/9831f.html#Heading3.

### Chapter 12: Focus Your Faith
[1] Benjamin Carson, with Gregg Lewis, *The Big Picture: Getting Perspective on What's Really Important in Life* (Grand Rapids, MI: Zondervan, 1999).
[2] Quotations taken from Jewel Diamond Taylor's Web site: www.jeweldiamondtaylor.com. To contact her for a speaking engagement, call (323) 964-1736.
[3] Ibid.

### Chapter 13: Hold On to Hope
[1] Morgan Scott Peck, *The Road Less Traveled* (New York: Simon & Schuster, 1978). For more of Peck's insights on this subject, see his section on "Discipline."
[2] See Iyanla Vanzant's, *One Day My Soul Just Opened Up: 40 Days and 40 Nights Towards Spiritual Strength and Personal Growth,* published by Fireside in 1998. Available on Amazon.com.
[3] The cartoon with this line appeared in 1971 on Earth Day. The comic creator of Pogo was Walt Kelly (1913–1973).
[4] Quotation from *As You Like It*, Act II, Scene 1.
[5] These lyrics are from the song "God Will Take Care of You." Words by Civilla D. Martin, 1904; music by W. Stillman Martin, 1904.

### Chapter 14: Make Your Move
[1] This poem is included at the end of Willie Jolley's book, *A Setback Is a Setup for a Comeback*, published by St. Martin's Press, 1999.

### Chapter 15: Don't Give Up
[1] Words and Music to "I Go to the Rock" by Dottie Rambo, 1977.

# OTHER POWERFUL BOOKS

## from Whitaker House

### Crazy House, Sane House
*George & Jeannie Bloomer*

There are two kinds of marriage you can end up with: good or bad, crazy or sane. The end result is up to you! If marriage is in your near future, or even if you've been married for decades, don't wait another minute! Discover the keys to building a strong house, a strong marriage, and a strong future!

ISBN: 0-88368-726-7 • Trade • 144 pages

### Even with My Issues
*Dr. Wanda A. Turner*

The enemy will try anything to prevent you from moving beyond your issues. But you can be free of the shame and bondage of your issues. Dr. Wanda Turner invites you on the most challenging journey you will ever take—a journey from rejection to acceptance, from fear to faith, from a shattered life to wholeness. Discover how you, too, can be entirely set free.

ISBN: 0-88368-673-2 • Trade • 160 pages

# OTHER POWERFUL BOOKS

## from Whitaker House

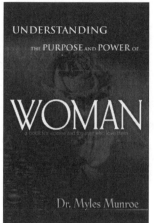

### Understanding the Purpose and Power of Woman
*Dr. Myles Munroe*

To live successfully in the world, women need to know what role they play. They need a new awareness of who they are, and new skills to meet today's challenges. Myles Munroe helps women to discover who they are. Whether you are a woman or a man, married or single, this book will help you to understand the woman as she was meant to be.

ISBN: 0-88368-671-6 • Trade • 208 pages

### Understanding the Purpose and Power of Men
*Dr. Myles Munroe*

Today, the world is sending out conflicting signals about what it means to be a man. Many men are questioning who they are and what roles they fulfill in life—as a male, a husband, and a father. Best-selling author Myles Munroe examines cultural attitudes toward men and discusses the purpose God has given them. Discover the destiny and potential of the man as he was meant to be.

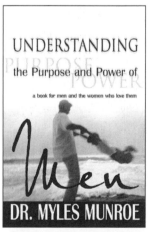

ISBN: 0-88368-725-9 • Trade • 224 pages